Angel EFT

Tap into the Angelic Realms with Modern Energy EFT

Susan Browne

First Edition 2016

DragonRising Publishing

United Kingdom

Angel EFT: Tap into the Angelic Realms with Modern Energy EFT
Text © Susan Browne
Energy EFT © Silvia Hartmann
All Rights Reserved In All Media.

ISBN: 978-1-908269-84-3

First Edition, v1.0

Published By
DragonRising Publishing
United Kingdom
www.DragonRising.com

Disclaimer

This book is aimed at helping people who have an interest in angels and Energy EFT to learn about the techniques of Angel EFT for personal development. It is intended to be informative and helpful for the readers well-being, and to provide knowledge about Energy EFT, Angels and Angel EFT.

This book is not intended to provide or replace medical advice. Energy EFT and particularly Angel EFT are still considered to be in an exploratory phase. The use of techniques by readers or those who learned about them via this book at all times remain responsible for their own well-being.

For Mum (Carol Yates)

My first teacher about the angels and energy

healing

Acknowledgements

Many thanks to Gary Craig who first gifted the world with EFT, and to Silvia Hartmann, the brilliant and dynamic founder of Energy EFT, whose technique is adopted in Angel EFT and works so well, and whose trainings and books I have so enjoyed and grown from. To Diana Cooper for the encouragement, and who has taught me and so many others how to work with angels. Much of the knowledge I have about the angels expressed in this book is courtesy of Diana Cooper. Many thanks to Zoe and the DragonRising Publishing team.

Thanks to Helen Ryle, my inspirational Kerry Energy EFT trainer, and mother hen, who urged me to follow through and get Angel EFT out there. I appreciate the loving encouragement I receive from my husband Thomas and the inspiration from my sons Dylan, Gerard and Elliott. Writing can be a somewhat antisocial business at times. Sam Black, long-time bestie who helped me. All of my friends and family who encouraged me and said 'you can do it,' - you know who you are.

Thanks to my dad Brian for his ongoing enthusiastic support, and mum Carol who taught me about energy and angels when I was small and listened to my painfully long stories at dinner time when I was growing up, without falling asleep. Thanks to all the wonderful people I have had the privilege to do Angel EFT with so far, and those who have inspired my work in so many ways.

Thank you to all the writers I befriended through Listowel Writing Group and Listowel Writers Week, for sharing, and teaching me so much, and for the laughs. Those of you who got your books published and won competitions, I was so happy for you *and* beneficially envious. Thanks to the many writing workshop and course tutors along the way for helping me to develop my writing and finally become an author. Thank you to the angels, Archangels, Ascended Masters and loving ancestors who made this book possible.

"To fly as fast as thought, to anywhere that is, you must begin by knowing that you have already arrived."

— Richard Bach, Jonathan Livingston Seagull

Foreword

I love the angels and have communicated with them for many years. So when Susan Browne asked me to write a foreword for her book Angel EFT: *Tap into the Angelic Realms with Modern Energy EFT,* I was intrigued by the concept. As soon as I started to read I was fascinated by the beautiful way the angelic energies connect with Energy EFT.

I had never fully understood Energy EFT, but with Susan's simple, clear instructions it was soon obvious to me how it works, and that Angelic EFT is a very powerful technique. The way she puts a positive focus on everything really appealed to me and I soon found myself pausing to practise the various tapping scripts she provides. And I was really surprised at the way my energy quickly felt clearer. Yes, it really works.

I thoroughly enjoyed and related to the case histories Susan shares from her extensive practise. She chooses a wide variety of examples and I shall be using some of them regularly and making up my own scripts. Because of my angel and ascension orientation I was very interested in how to tap in order to connect with the angels, and also to bring and anchor in the twelve ascension chakras. Many people are really helped by an active technique like tapping to link the physical and spiritual, and the angelic realms will use any opportunity to link with us.

As I read Susan's book it became very clear that tapping can be used to ameliorate any situation from personal problems to emotional and physical healing to spiritual advancement. I very much liked the way she uses it to help animals. I loved this inspirational book that blends two well-loved themes together, and I highly recommend it to help people and animals in every way possible.

- Diana Cooper

International Spiritual Author and Speaker
Specialist in Angels & Ascended Masters
Creator of the Diana Cooper Foundation
dianacooper.com

Contents

Silvia Hartmann and Energy EFT

Without Silvia Hartmann this book would not be possible. Modern Energy EFT, which is her creation, comprises the roots and trunk of the Angel EFT tree. Silvia was born in Germany in 1959 and has lived and worked in the United Kingdom since 1978. As well as Energy EFT Silvia developed and constructed Positive EFT, Project Sanctuary, The Genius Symbols, EMO Energy in Motion, Events Psychology and Modern Stress Management.

In 1998 Silvia Hartmann co-founded the world's first certifying body for modern energy work, The Guild of Energists (formerly known as The AMT). She also wrote the world's first book on EFT 'Adventures in EFT: The Essential Guide to Emotional Freedom Techniques' (DragonRising, 1998), which was ultimately replaced after eight editions in 2010 by her book 'Energy EFT.'

Silvia Hartmann continues to lead The Guild of Energists as chairperson and to evolve the Third Field of modern energy work. Silvia created the Energy EFT Master Practitioner Training in 2011. In 2014 the EMO Master Practitioner Qualification was added followed by the Project Sanctuary Master, thus creating a solid and wide reaching training structure for modern Energists.

As a modern energy researcher, her work has so far given us a new system to explain human behaviour and emotions, and a decoding for the language of metaphor. This remarkable lady, also an artist, continues to create, research, write, teach and inspire with outstanding model designs in theory and practise. I, Susan, am awed at her ability to write books and trainings so thoroughly and deeply, and yet in a way that makes absolute sense and is perfectly practical.

"Love without logic is insanity. And vice versa."

— Silvia Hartmann
President, Guild of Energists
SilviaHartmann.GoE.ac

Chapter 1: Introducing Angel EFT

Introducing Angel EFT

The two most effective healing influences on my life to date are working with the angelic realm and Classic Emotional Freedom Techniques (Classic EFT). It was a perfectly natural progression for me to combine these two approaches, which work effortlessly together. I discovered that when I tapped, the angel connection came easier. Intuition deepens - and when we raise our vibration, which is a natural result of EFT, we find it naturally simpler to sense and understand the angels. When I started doing tapping videos in 2012 I found that I intuitively incorporated some of the practices I had learned through my angel training.

When I came across Silvia Hartmann's Energy EFT I found it even more compatible for combining with angel work, as it is slower and more mindful, like the meditative way people tend to connect with angels. The *heart healing position*, and taking three deep breaths here at the start and end of each tapping round is one way I find this style of EFT perfect for angel work. The positive and empowering *set-ups* compliment the way I have learned to work with angels. The *SUE Scale* opens us up to miraculous possibilities and broadens the mind, from just removing a problem, to seeing its polar opposite (the positive) in a way that I feel the angels like to work with us. For this reason, when I say Angel EFT I really mean '*Angel Energy EFT.*' More about what all of these things mean later, for those who are new to Modern Energy EFT.

Just like all energy work and angel work, the techniques and examples I have set in this book continue to evolve. Those of you who are already familiar either with Energy EFT or angel work may enjoy the flexibility and creative approach. Individuals may be guided to use their own versions, perfectly matched to their intuitive needs. Some people prefer the surety of following things word for word, such as tapping scripts, which I have included throughout this book. In the true spirit of Energy EFT, if using these techniques, it's best bring in your own words.

A Little Word about Angels

Angels are beings of light sent from Source or God (I refer to these interchangeably), and have been around for thousands upon thousands of years. They do not belong to any religion although they feature in many, in some form and sometimes by another name. For example, in Buddhism angels are referred to as both devas, or celestial beings and dharmapalas, or dharma protectors. In Hinduism, spirit beings who act in a similar capacity to angels have various names including gandharvas, asuras and devas. Angels in Islam, or Malaikah, act as messengers and intermediaries from Allah to the world. In Judaism, the *Malachim* are messengers of God who help carry out Gods work and Gods plan. In Mormonism angels are ministering spirits and resurrected personages. Christianity recognises angels and Archangels and a whole hierarchy of angels.

Calling on angels for help doesn't take anything away from anyone else. Angels are always happy to help, and the more you ask, the stronger your connection will become to your angels. The angels don't mind if you are religious or not, or which religion you follow, if you follow one. They are here to help anyone who asks them. That's the important bit you need to remember, to *ask*. Under the law of free will the angels won't intervene unless a person asks. That is, unless you are in a life threatening situation and you are not meant to die yet, or be seriously injured as part of your journey. They can step in then.

You can ask the angels for someone else, I always feel that this helps even if the person in question would never acknowledge or have an interest in angels. However, the issue of free will still remains. If you are asking for angels to help someone who is being self-destructive, for example, they have every right to keep on being self-destructive and there is very little you or I or the angels can do about it other than just to keep holding them in the light. This means to think as positively as you can about somebody, whilst being real, not getting into the fear but rather focussing on their higher potential and natural state of divinity. Seeing the light in them.

Everyone has a guardian angel whether or not they ever recognise them. A guardian angel is by your side always, like a non-judgemental mentor, observing and supporting. Our angels whisper to us our highest possible path, and are happy to guide us with practical, everyday things. You can ask your angel for help with anything. Your angel doesn't think *'that's very trivial, I won't be giving any help with that,'* or *'how selfish, asking for more money, what a materialistic person,'* etc. These are human projections. Your angel wants you to be happy. If you ask for things that are not for your highest good, or that are somehow to the detriment of another person, they will step back, and guide you in another direction if you are so willing.

Angels are often depicted in artwork as having wings, or a halo. Some people see wings on angels. Other times they are seen as just having a huge light radiating around them. Angels do not have free will themselves as they are messengers of God or Source. Even though some angels are associated with being male or female, such as Archangel Michael, they are simply associations as angels do not have a sex or gender. In this book I will sometimes use 'he' or 'she' when referring to an angel or Archangel, but it is simply the predominant energy I am referring to. It also sounds a lot better, I think, than referring to an angel as 'it.'

How do I know if Angels are really there?

Most people cannot hear or see angels because they vibrate at such high frequency which is outside of most humans range at the time of writing this book. You can however *learn* to see, hear or sense angels. It is easier to connect with angels when your frequency is high. Our frequency is high when we are in a state of joy, open-heartedness, positivity and suchlike. Spiritually evolved and openhearted people can often naturally achieve a high vibration a lot of the time. Our vibration is ever changing, and it can be affected by things going on around us. The more consistent we get in keeping a high vibrational state the easier it is to be there. Old hurts and triggers, family patterns, spending time with negative people or organisations, and stressful life events can pull us back again.

The angels are always there for us no matter what our vibration is however the higher our vibrational state. However, the higher our vibration the easier we are to work with. Like attracts like. If you are in a bad mood and feeling pessimistic and resentful it will be harder to sense your angels. When you feel like you're stuck in the muck you are more likely to be negative with those around you, and your frequency naturally lowers. You might even contribute to lowering other people's frequency too, especially those close to you or affected by you. Of course there will be days that are challenging, no matter how many angels we implore. Challenges are sometimes needed for our growth. But the higher our frequency the better we cope with these trials. By anchoring our faith that everything is unfolding just as it is meant to, combined with taking sensible action, and focusing on gratitude, things work out easier for us and we are better able to get back on track.

How Do I Connect with the Angels?

You can ask the angels to help by simply addressing them out loud or in your mind. Many people have come across the so-called parking angels and are pleasantly surprised to find a parking space whenever they call on these angels. It might sound frivolous, but you really can ask the angels for pretty much anything. They like to help because when things go right for you, you naturally raise your frequency, and that is beneficial for everyone. The more people on the planet operating at a high frequency the better for each and every one. There are many different ways of sensing your angels' presence. These are only some, and your angel will pick the ones that you would be most alert to:

● Angel signs, like seeing an unexpected white feather after asking the angels for help. This can also be a deceased loved one carried by an angel. Hearing songs about angels, or beautiful music unexpectedly, and angel shapes in the clouds, or seeing certain numbers repeatedly.

● Clairaudience, hearing the voice of your angel. Unlike in psychotic illnesses, where the voices are often scary or lower frequency as the person sees into the lower astral planes, hearing the voices of angels is always uplifting. Some people hear voices like a thought inside their head; some hear it like an actual voice.

● Clairvoyance: seeing angels, either as an image in your head like a picture on a screen or actually seeing them with your physical eyes, just as you see objects normally. Angels appear differently according to the person and what makes sense to them.

● Clairsentience: having a feeling that your angel is there, some people feel great hands of light on their back or shoulders. Or it could be a sense that your angel is near.

● Claircognizance: clear knowing, you're not sure how you know an angel is there or is guiding you with something, but you just do, like a gut feeling.

● A beautiful scent or aroma, such as incense or flowers, without any apparent physical origin, particularly when you have been talking about, reading about or thinking about the angels.

I see angels in my mind's eye and they like to make me laugh. They do this to help keep my frequency light enough to connect, as laughter and humour literally lightens us up. I don't see them all the time, usually just if I ask or if I am meditating. I started to see them in around 2007 when I began to open up spiritually after being somewhat closed down for some years. I also sense or feel them. On two occasions, once in an angel workshop and another time when I was completing my Reiki Master training I could feel enormous hands of light on my shoulder blades and back, which I recognised to be the presence of an angel. I have also heard beautiful music whilst meditating and even while working in a hospital and been unable to decipher where it was coming from. Another time I smelled beautiful incense while reading an angel book on a plane awaiting departure. In meditations I have also smelled beautiful aromas like a divine scent of roses.

<u>Finding out the Name of Your Guardian Angel</u>

It is good to know what the name of your guardian angel is. That way you can call them by name, it makes it more personal. When I tried to do this in the beginning it took some time, because I kept getting different names each time I asked. This happens when either your angels name is changing, sometimes they change their name according to what's going on for you, or more likely I had quite a few angels working alongside my guardian angel and they were giving me their names. I know now what my guardian angels name is. If you get the name of an Archangel it is likely that your guardian angel is connected to that Archangel. The Archangels themselves cannot be guardian angels, but they can direct the guardian angels and link in with them.

You can ask your guardian angel to tell them your name whilst you meditate; you can use Energy EFT to open up to getting the name if you feel blocked or not confident about it. It will be easier to receive angel messages when you are relaxed and in a meditative state. There are many ways you can do this. I like to find somewhere quiet, light a candle and set my intention to connect to the angels and be open to their guidance.

When you work with angels, doors of opportunity open, healing can occur that you never thought possible and great things happen. [1]

What is EFT and Modern Energy EFT?

EFT stands for Emotional Freedom Techniques and is also sometimes called tapping. There are many different styles now but they all originate from its founder, Gary Craig, an engineer from the United States in the 1980's. Going back further, EFT's forerunner was thought field therapy (TFT) discovered by Roger Callahan when his patient's longstanding water phobia simply disappeared after tapping under her eye on the stomach meridian point. The energy meridians were first recognised in Eastern philosophy and therapies such as acupuncture, Reiki, Tai Chi, work with the chakras, Bio-energy and many, many more. I have included two chapters about the chakras; I have found knowing about them an asset to good health and spiritual growth.

The Energy EFT approach is to improve the flow of energy through the energy body by removing blockages at an energetic level. It is a treatment modality which belongs to the third field in the Mind, Body and Spirit triad. It is neither psychology nor physiology.

All humans have an energy body, and although we cannot see the energy body we recognise in Modern Energy EFT that it has a head of energy (the energy mind), hands made of energy (healing hands) and organs such as the heart centre. It has many channels which transport energy in through and out of the energy body.

➢ The energy must flow freely in order to work properly.

➢ Blockages can occur which stop the energy flowing freely.

---

1   To receive my free e-book '33 Ways to Connect & Work with Angels' go to bit.ly/Angel33ebook

➢ In Energy EFT we tap on meridian points to enhance the flow of energy and free up the blocks.

➢ As those blocks are freed up the person naturally feels revitalised and things change.

My own experience of Energy EFT for myself and with clients is that problems which seemed insurmountable don't seem all that bad at all, or are completely gone in terms of the distress they were causing. A sense of calm and relief is common. And when the distress is overcome and you move onto tapping into the positive as shown to us by Silvia Hartmann in Modern Energy EFT, you enhance or bring in the good rather than trying to get rid of the bad. Here the energy changes to a higher vibration and feelings of joy, harmony and delight are common.

In Hartmann's Energy EFT, the heart healing position was introduced. Rather than setting up on the karate chop point you take three deep, connecting breaths with hands over the heart centre. This in itself acts to stabilise and strengthen the entire energy body, and is returned to at the end of a tapping round. The tapping points have changed from classical EFT. The underarm point is omitted and the finger points are all included. It is slower than classical EFT, as a deep or comfortable breath is taken at each tapping point.

Additionally, Hartmann introduced the SUE Scale, a remarkable evolution of the traditional SUDS (Subjective Units of Distress) whereby we don't just tap to remove problems, but to keep going to get to the other side. So instead of pursuing 'zero' we look towards the pluses, up to +10. Silvia Hartmann encourages us not just to get ourselves into the plusses of the SUE Scale but to keep going for +10, which is a healing event, where she says the problem does not return.

The Sciencey Bit

EFT tapping sends signals directly to the stress centres of the midbrain, accessing the amygdala which is the integrative emotional centre of the brain, unlike in regular talking therapies, and so it allows a whole new way of working with trauma, for example. There is also evidence to suggest that EFT has a positive effect on cortisol levels. Cortisol is the 'stress hormone' and originally helped us to survive in the wild activating the fight or flight response. It is widely acknowledged that in modern day living we are often releasing cortisol too regularly due to stress, which has a negative effect on our physical, mental and emotional well-being.

Dr. Feinstein, a clinical psychologist using EFT in his own practice, stated that EFT is *"unusually precise, rapid, and direct for shifting the neurological underpinnings of a range of psychological problems."* Also that, *"the number of therapists using EFT has been rapidly increasing over the past decade, and now peer-reviewed research is showing that their instincts have been right. Surprisingly rapid outcomes with a variety of disorders are being documented."*

We don't know yet all of the things that EFT can help, and why EFT will help one person with a symptom and not another, but we know that it has made a massive impact on healing in the world to date. For me, I will try it on anything. Where I cannot teach a person to tap, or tap on them, or for an animal or situation, I can proxy tap - where you tap on behalf of someone else, or an animal or situation. It is pretty impossible to measure whether proxy tapping works or not, but at the very least, and I have seen amazing results which I believe are due to proxy tapping, it makes the tapper feel calmer and more proactive. They are doing something positive with their intention instead of worrying which only feeds the energy of fear. More about this in Chapter 10.

As always, if you are a professional working with clients, remember not to make any claims of cure. Take the attitude of 'I have this really helpful technique that could help the energy around this situation, if you'd like we could try it.' Be professional. Also, not everyone wants to work with angels, yet. Not all of my clients do. You can still always ask the angels to guide you in your work, but use your intuition and common sense as to whether to introduce Angel EFT in your EFT practise or not. You might find, that since you have an interest in angels, you will attract many clients who also do, but do not presume that all of them do. Having an angel picture, figurine, book, cards etc in your workplace might prompt your client to express an interest in angels, if they have one.

How to Use This Book

You can read this book chronologically or it's fine to jump to chapters that really resonate for you or somebody you are working with. I have created some symbols to prompt you with certain reminders, instead of repeating text over and over.

De-stressing before starting a tapping round

If you are feeling really stressed, in the minuses of the SUE Scale, it's always worth doing a de-stressing round first. You can invoke the angels in your de-stress round if you wish, either mentally before you begin or by using an angel word in your round, such as tapping on 'angels of peace,' or 'angels of calm.'

When you see the above symbol it is a reminder to check in and see if you need to start with a de-stressing round.

When you see this symbol:

It means use your own wording as needed. I put this where I have written a suggested tapping script. I cannot advocate the right tapping words for someone who is not in front of me, explaining precisely what they'd like to work on in their own words. No two humans are the same and the same is true of what they'd like to work on with Energy EFT. Sometimes you might read the script and say 'yes that's me, the wording is just fine,' but other times it might not fit, and you can say the words that work best for you.

I write sample EFT rounds as just one round. In Energy EFT this is normally considered quite short. This is because often the second round is similar to the first or if it is different it is because it has evolved as something further has been uncovered. So not wanting to be repetitive or to try to predict the evolution for everyone I have just written them all as one round. Please if you are using my words…. *keep tapping beyond that one round as needed, even if you are just repeating it.*

This is the symbol I will sometimes use to remind you of this:

Using the SUE (Subjective Units of Experience) Scale

Please use the SUE Scale – illustrated in Chapter 2. It is so helpful in terms of charting your progress. The SUE Scale helps you to monitor where you are at, how you are feeling, how you are progressing with your energy work. In Angel EFT it works in the same way. You can either ask the question 'where am I on the SUE Scale just now?' This focuses on your energy body and thus emotions generally. It's like a global 'how am I doing?' question. Or, you can apply it to what you are tapping for, for example: 'how abundant do I feel right now on the SUE Scale?' The SUE Scale is another reminder to keep going with your energy work. If you have come from a minus 4 to a plus 2, why stop there? The SUE Scale is a great reminder to keep on evolving, until you are at plus 10 which is an event, and anchors the change. I put this symbol in periodically just as a reminder:

This is the symbol I use to remind you about the power of the heart healing position, where we set up and complete a round of Energy EFT:

You can use this point (referred to in this book as 'HC' for heart centre, to simply tune in, to recharge when your energy is low and as part of your Energy EFT work as described. I made the symbol to emphasise the power of this point, and the wisdom and insights you get from spending some time here, taking three or more mindful breaths.

Make sure that you read the chapter on Modern Energy EFT if you are not familiar. It is different to Classical EFT. There is nothing to stop you doing Angel EFT with classical protocols by the way, if that's your preferred technique. I am a convert who used to use classical, and nowadays find Modern Energy EFT fits better. It feels more mindful and compatible with Angel EFT to me. I also have huge respect and deep gratitude towards the many classical EFT Masters and Practitioners I have learned so much from along the way.

What's the difference between Angel EFT and ordinary Energy EFT?

Angel EFT uses the same principles mostly as Energy EFT, with the same tapping points. In Angel EFT we are asking the angels to join us in our healing work. Sometimes we use it to call in the assistance of the angels, or a specific angel or Archangel. We use visualisations at times also, with angels, to help heal, clear or create new energy. We can also adopt the usual Energy EFT protocol, and simply use words added to our usual method, such as 'I invite my angels to help with this now.' The word 'angel' has a high vibrational energy, and speaking about angels, thinking about them, reading about them etc. often has the effect of raising a person's energy vibration. Angel EFT is another type of Energy EFT and can be used as well as the original form, and even interchangeably. It will appeal to those who already love both angels and energy work, and who naturally want to connect to the angelic realms.

Frequency and Dimensions

You will hear me talk about frequency and dimensions in this book, I use them almost interchangeably although they are not the same. The frequency you are vibrating at refers to your state of being at a particular moment in time. Think of the frequency as being like a radio airwave, and the frequency you are vibrating at, or operating at. What frequency are you vibrating at just now? Here are just some of what we humans can resonate with...

Misery & Fear   **Gossip & Drama**   **Discontent**

Gratitude   **Meditation & Angels**   **Joy & Fun**

If we are operating at a high frequency we are feeling good, things are typically going well for us which is a reflection from the outer of the inner. Lower frequency ways of being are fear based.

Fear in humans manifests in any number of ways, but you can get good at spotting it and choose not to subscribe or join in if you wish. Fear behaviours include: doom and gloom talk, complaining, anxiety, mistrustfulness, ego stuff, wanting material things to out-do others or feel superior, rather than for enjoying the richness and variety of life. There are plenty of things on TV and in the media that are lower frequency and fear based. Take the news for example, yes okay it's the news, but why don't they tell us the good things that are happening too? Fear is still selling newspapers.. at the time of writing anyhow.

The dimensions that we typically experience in this human experience just now are:

Third Dimension: fear based, no concept of ourselves as a spiritual being of light. Self-centred.

Fourth Dimension: waking up and opening up to our*selves* and the support available to us. Appreciating the 'coincidences' as synchronicity.

<u>Fifth Dimension:</u> Oneness consciousness; the knowing that we are all connected and everything we do has a ripple effect on the whole. This is primarily the highest dimension we can maintain whilst in a human body. Here we easily connect with angels, and we are operating at a high frequency. We are open-hearted and see the higher perspective in situations, and the higher potential of people even if their actions are displeasing.

Many people have remained in third dimension for many, many generations but now people are waking up and many people have moved into fourth, and every day more and more are achieving a fifth dimensional state. It can be a challenge to maintain when surrounded by others' operating at a lower frequency, and the collective consciousness is just rubbing the sleep out of its eyes while I am writing this. But this is all changing, and more and more people are awake than have been for a very long time.

<u>Case Examples</u>

I use Case Examples in this book which are based on real clients and experiences. Witnessing what Angel EFT can do has been my inspiration for writing this book. However, for the protection of privacy I have changed the details comprehensively.

Chapter Summary:

● Angel EFT is the natural combination of working with angels and Energy EFT. There are many ways in which you can do this and there are no hard and fast rules.

● Although angels have been associated with religion they are not exclusive to religions and are there for everyone.

● Calling on the angels for help doesn't take away from anyone else, and nothing is too trivial to ask for help with. Angels don't judge.

● By asking the angels for help you are in turn raising your frequency, which is beneficial to all as the more people raising their frequency on the planet the better for everyone.

● Everyone has a guardian angel that stays with them throughout their life whether or not they ever acknowledge this.

● The more we raise our frequency the easier it is for angels to make themselves known to us and guide us.

● Everyone has free will and angels will only step in to help if they are asked or in the case of an emergency.

● Clairaudience, clairvoyance, clairsentience, claircognizance, angel signs such as feathers and clouds, music and beautiful aromas are some of the ways we can experience the presence of our angels.

● EFT stands for Emotional Freedom Techniques and originates from Gary Craig, a Stanford Engineer and beyond that from Eastern Practises of energy healing.

● Modern Energy EFT was created by Silvia Hartmann and is the central EFT approach behind Angel EFT in this book.

● The aim of Energy EFT is to improve the flow of energy through the energy body by removing blockages at an energetic level.

● All humans have an energy body and the energy must flow freely within it in order to work properly.

● Energy EFT can be tried on everything.

● If you are a therapist or work with clients, don't make any claims of cure. Always be professional. Introduce angels if you understand your client wants this.

● Angel EFT can be used in both classical and Modern Energy EFT protocols; however the Modern Energy EFT is slower and more mindful and is the way I choose to teach Angel EFT.

● Make sure you are familiar with the tapping protocols before you begin.

● Your frequency refers to your state of being at a particular time, in high frequency we can easily connect with angels and things tend to go well for us. We see the higher perspective of what is occurring and our role in it, instead of being frightened or outraged by it.

● The dimensions humans operate in are third, fourth and fifth. At fifth dimension we can easily work with angels, we don't subscribe to fear-based thinking and we acknowledge oneness.

Summary of Symbols

Symbol	Meaning
◯	De-stress first as needed before working on the issue.
(heart with pen in speech bubble)	Use your own wording as needed, my words in tapping scripts are only a guideline and don't apply to everyone. In the true spirit of modern Energy EFT, we don't advocate words for people to use, we encourage people to always use their own words. Angel EFT is a specific branch of modern Energy EFT and to help people get confident in it I use the suggested rounds in this book (as well as tapping videos on YouTube and Facebook) simply to help people in getting started.
(circular arrow with face)	Remember to repeat rounds, tap for longer, use your own words as the work evolves.
(ruler/scale)	Remember to use the SUE Scale.
(heart with wings)	Hands on heart centre or heart healing position, feel your healing hands and really tune in to what is going on for you. We do this at the beginning and end of each round, it is centring and grounding and will help you to gain more insight. Pause here and allow the energy to settle.

Chapter 2: How to Do Modern Energy EFT

Changes from Classical to Modern Energy EFT

There are a few differences in Modern Energy EFT to classical EFT and some are mentioned in Chapter 1. The *set-up* has changed and some of the tapping points. In classical EFT we set up by tapping on the side of the hand and stating the problem with an 'even though,' before it and an 'I deeply love and accept myself,' after it, or words to that effect. For example, 'even though I feel overwhelmed at work, I deeply love and accept myself.' In the heart and soul protocol, the set-up is at the heart centre, or heart healing position and we simply state the problem, e.g.) 'Overwhelmed at work.' This is to keep very focused on the issue at hand, and not get side-tracked by arguments for a client who may feel perturbed by having to say they deeply love and accept themselves when they do not feel as though they do. The scale for rating a problem and measuring progress is also different, previously SUD's, in Modern Energy EFT becomes the SUE.

The Energy EFT Heart & Soul Protocol

Setting Up

Place the hands on the centre of the chest (the heart healing position) and take three comfortable breaths stating the problem or the issue you are working on. I will refer to this point for the rest of this book as HC (heart centre).

The Tapping Points

The next point is the top of the head (TH) - the crown point, where you can use a few or all of the fingers to tap
third eye point in the centre of the forehead (TE) using one or two fingers; the eyebrow point is the inner end of the eyebrow (EB); side of the eye is on the bony part just level with your pupil at the side of the eye (SE); under the eye is on the bone again directly under the eye (UE); under the nose is the point in the middle of under your nose and your top lip; under the mouth I refer to as CH as it is the inner crease part of the chin under the mouth; CB is collar bones where I tend to use all the fingers again to tap; top of the thumb is usually just with two fingers tapping (Th); top of the index finger (If); top of the middle finger (Mf); top of the ring finger (Rf); top pf the baby finger (Bf); then the side of the hand or Karate Chop Point where I use up to three fingers (KC) and back to having the hands on the centre of the chest (HC) taking three comfortable breaths again, unless you are continuing on the same round in which case you can go straight to the top of the head again.

De-Stressing First

It's a good idea when you are working on a problem to check in if you are feeling stressed (usually reflected in the SUE Scale as being in the minuses, see overleaf). If a person is stressed and they start tapping on the issues sometimes they end up going off on tangents and tapping on 'stress talk.' This is where we see things in a really bleak way. An example might be 'I am so upset with my partner, he never shows any affection, and my father never showed any affection when I was a child, nobody loves me, I always have these problems,' and so on. If you are really stressed out it is most effective to de-stress before beginning tapping on the issue you would like to work on. You can de-stress by choosing a word meaningful to you that you will tap on following the heart and soul protocol as described. Words that people have used include 'peace; calm; tranquil; restful; centred; grounded,' etc. Pick just one word and do a round on that or more as required.

Energy EFT

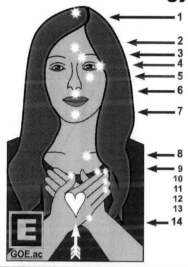

The Energy Points

0 – Heart Position

1 – Top of the head

2 – Third Eye point
3 – Top of the eyebrow
4 – Corner of the eye
5 – Under the eye
6 – Under the nose
7 – Under the mouth
8 – Collarbone point

9 – Thumb
10 – Index finger
11 – Middle finger
12 – Ring finger
13 – Little finger
14 – Karate Chop point

0 – Heart Position

SUE Scale Hartmann 2009

- Check the SUE Scale and pick a number.
- 0 - The Heart Position. Point to yourself in the centre of your chest. Place your leading hand over this point, then place your other hand on top. Take three deep breaths, in and out. Say out aloud what you will be tapping on. For example: I want more energy.
- 1 – 14 - Now tap all the points lightly, starting at the top of the head and ending with the Karate Chop point. Use the index finger of your leading hand. Pause between each point and take one deep breath in and out.
- 0: Return to the Heart Position and take three deep breaths in and out.
- Check the SUE Scale.
- Tap more rounds of Energy EFT until you get to +10.

Energy EFT On A Page – Created by Silvia Hartmann for The Guild of Energists GOE.ac
Translated by your local energist.

33

The Words

You can use whatever wording you like but starting off it is advisable to keep things as simple as possible. You can get fancy as you get more confident. Why not simply tap on the word 'angel' or 'energy' and see how you feel after it?

Remember...

● Tap lightly, think of closing a circuit.

● You can tap, massage or hold the points depending on your preference. In Angel EFT it is often useful to simply hold the points.

● Slow down.... because most people moving from classical EFT to Modern Energy EFT find the slower pace strange at first and end up moving from point to point more speedily than is required in this style of tapping.

The SUE Scale

We use the SUE Scale (Subjective Units of Experience) to rate the experience in terms of its distress or how positive it is. Unlike the SUDS used in classical EFT which deals in minuses and stops at zero, the SUE Scale encourages us to keep going up into the positives. Instead of just removing a problem, progress into its opposite. So for example, we can move from:
-6 feel so nervous about the driving test, to:
+6 so confident now.. I am really excited about doing the test so that I'll be a qualified driver Why not use the SUE Scale now for measuring something you'd like to work on with Energy EFT, for example, 'I'd love to work with the angels more and receive signs that they are with me.' Place your finger over the scale and slide it across until you feel the right number for you. If you are in the minuses you probably don't feel connected to the angels and are worried or upset about it. If you are in the positives, you feel excitement and joy about increasing your angel experiences and the associated blessings. Zero is neutral, or the 'zero point of peace.' When we increase the energy flow into the positive

side of the scale we are moving towards the healing event. The healing event anchors the change into the energy system. With each problem there is a parallel healing event. We don't have to come to the healing event in an initial Energy EFT session; any move in the right direction is progress. Also the set-up will change when we move from the minuses to zero to correspond with the new Energy EFT goal which is the healing event.

<u>Energy EFT Heart & Soul Technique</u>

1) **De-Stress**: Place your hands on the centre of your chest and take three deep breaths, slowly in and out. Do 2-3 rounds starting at the top of the head and finishing on the karate chop point, saying "relax" or "calm" whilst tapping/touching/massaging each point. Take a deep breath in and out before moving onto the next treatment point.

2) **Describe the problem** and how you feel as you think about it (the set-up statement) – e.g. "I never seem to have enough money", "I never have time to meditate", "I am so anxious about the meeting", "I don't feel motivated to exercise".

3) **Become aware** of any uncomfortable sensations as you tune into the problem; if the sensation had a colour, what would it be?

4) **Take a SUE Scale reading** – on a scale of -10 to +10, -10 being the worst pain/fear/sadness/despair imaginable and +10 being the best and most alive and positive you could ever feel when focusing on this issue.

5) **Tap 1-3 rounds**, beginning with heart healing as above, and repeat a reminder phrase on each point, e.g. 'not enough money,' 'they talk about me,' 'anxious about the meeting,' 'no motivation to exercise.'

6) **Check how you feel on the SUE Scale** as you focus again on the issue. Continue with tapping rounds focusing on the problem until you are at zero when you think about it.

7) **Then do a further 2-3 rounds focusing on the positive** emotions you would like to feel when you think of the issue/person/event/memory. You can use single words or short phrases: 'free-flowing abundance,' 'confident and calm,' 'bliss,' 'amazing competence,' 'super motivated to exercise.'

And that's it! As simple as that. No need to worry about getting it wrong or getting the wrong statement, all the Energy EFT you do is good for you. This works for physical sensations, and for emotions and even for beliefs that may be a problem too.

Images & Concepts based on Energy EFT by Silvia Hartmann GOE.ac

Want to see Susan demonstrating Energy EFT and Angel EFT? Visit the 'Angel EFT Lady' YouTube Channel at http://bit.ly/SusanYTube

Chapter Summary:

● The set-up begins at the heart centre where we contact the problem by stating it.

● Take a deep or comfortable breath between each tapping point.

● Check if you need to de-stress first before beginning tapping and do a round to de-stress if needs be.

● Use the SUE Scale to measure how progress is going, and to think 'beyond zero,' e.g. towards a healing event which is the corresponding opposite of the problem.

● Move your set-ups into positive ones as problems subside, for example 'feeling drained,' could become 'even more energy.'

Chapter 3: Combining Energy EFT with Angel Work

There are many different ways we can call upon angels to help us out in our lives or to help others. I have had a lot of fun trying out different ways, and Angel EFT will continue to develop. The techniques I describe are just some of the ways you can bring the angels into your Energy EFT practise.

Different Angel EFT Techniques in a nutshell

I describe nine main techniques in this book that you can use in Angel EFT. These can be successfully combined as needed:

1) Visualising with the angels prior to tapping
2) Visualising with the angels after tapping
3) Tapping on the name of an angel
4) Address the angels in your Energy EFT round
5) Visualise the angels tapping with you
6) Ask the angels to supercharge your healing hands with golden energy prior to tapping
7) Angel prayer tapping
8) Angel cards with Energy EFT
9) Crystal angel tapping

1) Visualising with the angels prior to tapping

Complete a visualisation with the angels, it could be twenty minutes or more or even just a few moments. An example might be cord cutting with Archangel Michael:

Visualisation Example: Place your feet flat on the floor and take some deep calming breaths. Be aware of your feet and imagine sending down thick golden roots that reach all the way to the centre of the earth, dipping into a pool of light. From the pool of light accept healing which travels lovingly back up the roots and into your physical body. Allow this healing light into every cell in the body and feel yourself lighting up.

Now imagine that from above your head flows a stream of golden light, it flows into the energy body, allowing it into all the chakras and flowing easily through all the energy meridians. Allow yourself to fully relax and enjoy this powerfully calming energy that easily flows through your body.

Ask Archangel Michael to place you in a deep blue bubble of light which helps you to feel very safe.

Call in your angels, your guardian angel and any of the angels or Archangels you like working with or desire assistance from.

Your guardian angel is bringing you to a very peaceful place with mountains and a shimmering lake in a valley. You find yourself at the lake shore and Archangel Michael is with you. You feel very relaxed and protected as this beautiful great figure, with gold and blue light emanating out greets you. He tells you he is going to assist you with some energy clearing. He pulls out from the lake a large mirror and places it in front of you. You can see yourself in the mirror but also you may become aware of energy cords which are attaching you to other people or memories or things in an unhealthy way, draining your energy. These cords are quite common, but reduce our energy and with Archangel Michael's help we can cut these, without it being to the detriment of anyone else. We have cords between us and people we resent, but also between us and loved ones sometimes. Cutting the cords doesn't mean cutting the person off, it is simply cutting off any toxic energy exchange, which is a helpful thing for all concerned. So if you are aware of some cords that you have, Archangel Michael allows you to use his sword of light to cut the cords now. You may feel a big release as you cut through the cords, as this greatly frees up your energy. Take deep breaths and be aware of light that is sent to each recipient of the cords when they are cut, and they dissolve healthily away. Take some time here; be open to any messages or guidance from the angels about how to mind your energy in the future. Some of the cords can occasionally be hard to cut through, for whatever reason. If you have any that seem hard to cut right now just place the very tip of the sword of light onto the cord, and see it being shrunk down to a more manageable size, with much less toxic exchange. You may feel more empowered the next time to cut it completely.

When you are finished you hand back the sword to Archangel Michael and Archangel Raphael steps forward. He emanates a beautiful emerald green energy, and he places a sparkling green energy salve on any places in your energy body where you cut the cords, so that these areas are filled with healing light. Take some deep cleansing breaths as you feel your energy body light up even more with this healing light from Archangel Raphael. See your energy self in the mirror now, clear and bright and radiant looking. This is how you look to the angels. Thank the two Archangels now and come away with your guardian angel, who brings you gently back into the room. Take your time bringing your awareness back into the room. Open your eyes slowly.

Still with eyes closed imagine your energy body as a shining light, see yourself looking confident and assured. Breathe in the energy for a few more moments and allow it to settle. Remember the roots you sent down, keeping you grounded and secure. Gently open your eyes and check in. Place your hands on your heart centre and focus on what you learned in the visualisation.[2]

One lady became aware of a large cord which was attached from her solar plexus to her father, whom she had a fractious relationship with. The following round was helpful for her after this visualisation in words that were meaningful to her…

---

2   My newsletter subscribers receive a free audio download of the above visualisation at http://bit.ly/freeangelvis

HC Set-up: I want to release the pain and resentment around Dad

TH: I release this resentment towards Dad with the help of my angels

TE: Dad is responsible for his behaviour in life

EB: Releasing any fears around this now

SE: And I am responsible for mine

UE: I release the hurt now as it no longer serves me

UN: Dad can choose to behave however he wants

CB: I have the power to be who I want to be

Th: Sending love to my relationship with Dad

If: I am open to a healthy energy exchange with Dad

Mf: Any toxic energy from Dad flows in through and out

Rf: It doesn't leave any debris any more

Bf: My energy is healthy and full of light

KC: And I send love to all the former aspects[3] of myself that felt hurt by Dad

Three deep breaths at heart centre

HC: Thank you Archangels Michael and Raphael

HC: Thank you higher self for this anchored new wisdom

Then she intuitively went into a positive round using the words 'healthy happy energy.' The visualisation had shown her the biggest 'cord' of fear, and she was then able to tap on what came up.

---

3   Aspects are mentioned throughout this book, which refers to Silvia Hartmann's Aspects Model. Instead of talking about earlier versions of me or a client or future me's in Modern Energy EFT we call all of these 'aspects'. Each of these aspects you can think of as a snap shot of the precise conditions in the energy system at that particular time. The aspect of you who woke up this morning is already a different aspect to the you who is reading these words. When we use the Aspects Model we have the choice to go into being the aspect again, re-living the experience, or more favourably to observe as though a third party, which helps to avoid abreactions, which is to re-experience the distress as the repressed emotion is released.

<u>One FAQ about visualisations:</u>

What if I can't see/feel anything during my visualisation?

I have taught and attended many angel workshops, and participants have so many different experiences during the visualisations. Some people are very visual and report wonderful colours, messages, sensations from the visualisation. And others are looking perplexed in hearing this, saying 'I felt or saw nothing, how do I know it worked?' Well the answer is in the intention. If you ask the angels for help, expect that they will do so. If you ask Archangel Michael to help cut cords, consider it done. Your spiritual gifts might be very different to the person sitting beside you, and they might open up even more as time goes on. Try not to compare yourself to others as it can be disheartening and lead to unhelpful thoughts which draw your vibration down and make you harder to connect with. Use Angel EFT to overcome any worries about it.

2) Visualising with the Angels after Tapping

After tapping we are naturally more open to our angels, our energy is lighter and we are easy to connect with. Simply close your eyes and imagine the angel or angels you want to work with surrounding you. Be open to their guidance, and curious as to how it might arrive. Sometimes guidance comes later in the day, through a sign that you will recognise if you stay open, or in dream time.

Case Example: After doing a round of tapping for money Steven visualised connecting with Archangel Gabriel, asking the Archangel Gabriel to light up in his aura any symbols to do with money that he should know about. He intuitively saw little whirlpools that were small from the inside and vacuuming out at the edge of his aura. He said that this matched his belief that he wasn't good with money, and that money simply slips through his fingers. He said 'even when I do receive money I get rid of it fast.' He asked the angels to reverse the flow of the whirlpools in his aura so that instead of money being pulled out and away from him he would instead draw it in towards him.

He then became aware of another limiting belief and he said 'but I don't want to hoover other people's money away from them.' We talked about this and he uncovered that he had this other limiting belief that maybe he wasn't a good healer, and when he did get clients he was just conning people out of their money. The evidence was that this was far from the truth; he was a very caring and conscientious energy healer who always went out of his way for his clients. So we did another round of Positive EFT[4] on 'my clients get much more than the cash value - my healing work is very far reaching.' He was not resistive to this and right away his energy lifted. He remembered all the people he had helped and all the positive feedback he had received. He also remembered he had received some good testimonials which he had been meaning to use and not got around to doing. He made plans to deal with that right away after the session. We finished with a couple more rounds on deserving money, and 'aura that attracts money'. He went into the visualisation again and saw his aura looking bright and healthy with whirlpools that now attract and welcome the flow of money.

Visualising with the angels after tapping also acts to anchor the new concept: Adrianna had a lot of anger towards the schooling system. To say the word school made her feel so angry and resentful it scored -35 on the SUE Scale. We did some tapping and after just a few rounds she had reached a +8 on the SUE Scale. We then did a brief visualisation to anchor her new progress. It went like this:

Gently close your eyes and tune into this new feeling. Ask your guardian angel to step closer into your aura and notice any sensations or a sense of connection. Imagine when you are breathing in you are breathing in the colour gold and this gold light is filling up each cell in the body. Filling up the aura so that you feel light and peaceful, and confident in assuming this new peaceful feeling around the words associated with school. Your angels are supporting you with this healthy new change. Choose an image of something beautiful or peaceful that you will now associate with words associated with school. Light it up in your mind as you anchor this new connection. Lighting up the subconscious mind and allowing this peaceful feeling to flow to you in all directions of time.

---

4   Positive EFT, created by Silvia Hartmann works with positive Set Up statements using Energy EFT. By increasing energy flow on what we wish for in life rather than focusing on what we want to get rid of or reduce, we can unlock our own potential easily.

Take a few deep centring breaths. Wriggle your fingers and toes and when you are ready open your eyes.

Adrianna had an image of a beautiful mountain and lake. We tested the word school by way of my using it in various contexts, and her score remained +8.

3) Tapping on the Name of an Angel

You can call in an angel or Archangel, or connect with their energy while you tap by using the name of the angel. Simply tap or hold the points as in Energy EFT, say the name of the angel you wish to connect with. This is a great round on its own but you can also go on to tap on what it is you want the angel to assist you with. For example, you might say 'Archangel Michael,' and then 'courage.'
Angel EFT for courage with Archangel Michael

Three deep breaths at heart centre
HC: Archangel Michael. Courage
TH: Archangel Michael
TE: Courage
EB: Archangel Michael
SE: Courage
UE: Archangel Michael
UN: Courage
CH: Archangel Michael
CB: Courage
Th: Archangel Michael
If: Courage
Mf: Archangel Michael
Rf: Courage
Bf: Archangel Michael
KC: Courage
HC: Archangel Michael. Courage.

You can quite simply tap (or hold or massage the points) saying the name of an angel or angels. Here are some examples:

- Archangel Michael

- Archangel Raphael

- Archangel Gabriel

- Archangel Haniel

- Archangel Uriel (for a more extensive list of the Archangels and what they may be helpful with see page...)

- Angels of nature

- Angels of travel

- Angels for parenting

- Angels for abundance

- Angels of love

- Angels for a beautiful home

- Shopping angels (seriously, I use these all the time and find what I want quickly getting the best bargains!)

- Angels for world peace

- Angels of the Violet Flame

- Creativity angels

- Presentation angels

- Angels for calm

- Angels of colour

- Angels for Fibromyalgia

- Angels of my workplace

- Angels for a healthy relationship

- Angels for good communication

4) Address the Angels in your Energy EFT Round

When we talk about angels in a positive way we are raising our frequency and this is no exception while we are tapping. An example of addressing the angels in an Energy EFT round would be if we were to call on Archangel Jophiel for opening the crown chakra to higher energies and to help with making the home beautiful. We might say:

Three deep breaths at heart centre
HC: Archangel Jophiel I want to make my home beautiful
TH: Thank you for bringing more light into my crown centre
TE: Allowing the highest light to flow through me now
EB: Lifting my thoughts and behaviours

SE: And giving me lots of inspiration for making my home tidy, orderly and delightful

UE: I release any patterns now about holding onto clutter in my mind, body or environment

UN: Thank you Archangel Jophiel for helping me to do this with ease

CH: Easily tidying and sorting things, letting go of things I don't need any more

CB: Feeling light and happy in my energy as I do this

Th: And bringing light and inspiration into my home

If: Angelic energy and inspiration into my home

Mf: Easy for me to tidy

Rf: Making my home beautiful

Bf: Releasing those feelings of overwhelm that have been holding me back

KC: Thank you Archangel Jophiel

Three deep breaths at heart centre

HC: Thank you for my beautiful tidy home

How might this evolve now? What do you need to feel more confident and ready to make your home beautiful? Use a Positive EFT approach, using a simple positive word, a quality you would like to experience and finish at HC by saying 'thank you Archangel Jophiel.'

Why do we thank the angels in advance?

Saying 'thank you angels' is a way of manifesting (because you are talking as though it has already happened) and also appreciating that the angels are already on board, because we have asked them, even if we are not yet seeing results.

For somebody going for a job interview they might call in a number of Archangels:

Three deep breaths at heart centre

Take your time at the heart centre here, best if you can close your eyes for part of it as you invoke each Archangel

HC: Archangel Michael heal and balance my throat centre now so that I may speak with self-assurance and courage

TH: Archangel Gabriel fill me with the pure light of clarity so that I may think clearly

TE: Archangel Uriel help me to access the wisdom and knowledge I need for this interview

EB: Archangel Raphael help me to visualise myself doing a great job in the interview

SE: Archangel Haniel please help me to be calm and confident

UE: I allow myself to shine at the interview

UN: I trust that you know what's best for me

CH: I trust that what's for me won't pass me

CB: And I know that you are helping me to be the best that I can be today

Th: The best that I can be in the interview

If: Thank you angels for helping me to release fears and self-doubt

Rf: If this job is for me then I'll certainly get it

Bf: Just as I won't get it if it's not for me

KC: I trust in the wisdom of the universe

HC: Feeling calm and confident in the interview with the help of the angels

Check in after this round and make a note of anything that came up for you. If you had a negative experience in an interview, or a situation that being in an interview reminds you of (having to speak in class or suchlike) do another round specific to that. Ask the angels to bring healing into that initial event.

5) Visualise the angels tapping with you

For those who are used to visualising, why not visualise that as you tap the angels are tapping on you as well? Imagine each tapping point lighting up as the angels work on you as well. I used to feel the angels were doing this anyway which was a major factor on my inspiration for Angel EFT. Energy EFT makes you more accessible to the angels, so it makes sense that they can tap along with you too.

6) Ask the angels for super charged golden healing hands before you begin tapping

Look down at your hands and raise them up, palms up as far as is comfortable. Ask the angels out loud or in your mind to bless your hands with the colour gold, or another colour if you prefer but gold is the colour of the angelic realm. Bring your hands back down in front of you and spend a few moments before tapping just receiving this light. See your hands in your mind's eye glowing with light; you may be aware of them tingling. Everybody has healing hands, asking the angels to bless them with gold light gives them an extra boost.

7) Angel prayer tapping

Tap or hold the points using prayer. Here is a general example of the type of words you could use but feel free to use your own wording always. If you use more traditional prayers, they also work very compatibly with Energy EFT.

Angels I receive your love
I accept your love
I offer forgiveness to myself and to others
Because with love I can do this
I expand love, I radiate love
I show love to all I come across
I open myself up to your gifts and your guidance

8) Using Angel Cards with Angel EFT

Angel cards are a useful way to connect with the angels, and can be combined with using Energy EFT. Choose a deck that resonates with you. There are lots out there and many are available as apps on the phone or tablet as well as a physical card deck.

Have a question in mind, something in your life that you would like guidance for perhaps. If you don't have anything specific you can simply ask 'angels, what would you like me to know today?' Hold the deck of cards in your hands, tap them three times (to clear the energy of whoever was using them last, or the issue you were dealing with if it was you) and mentally ask your question. Hold the cards to your heart centre and breathe a few breaths as you focus on your question. Pull a card and try to get out of your left brain of logic and reasoning for a moment, use your right brain of intuition which is the part we use initially for picking up angel messages. If the card has an image on, focus on the image instead of the words for a few moments, because when we focus on the words we are using the left brain.

Close your eyes then and tune in and see what comes up for you. Some people will find this easy where others will not. If nothing comes don't worry, it might be easier the next time. Sometimes we have to strengthen our intuition by practising using it. Just like going to the gym for the first time in a long time. As young children everyone's intuition worked perfectly well. It was society and conditioning that made many of us shut it down. The good news is; you can get it back again.

So if the card is meaningful you can then do a round of Energy EFT to enhance the message of the card or to connect in with the wisdom. A lady was asking about her career and getting her business off the ground. She worked as a Reiki healer, and she got the card 'counsellor' Archangel Raziel. The image showed a beautiful angel with one hand in the air and a torch in the other, and the message was about helping people with bereavements. She said many of the clients that came to her were suffering bereavements and she spent a lot of time talking to them after the reiki treatments. The card affirmed this and helped her to know that the work she was doing was meaningful. When we tapped on the positives of what she was already doing she began to get a flow of ideas of what she wanted to do to enhance her practise even more. She wanted to get a new healing space and the ideas began to flow.

9) Crystal Angel Tapping

Sometimes I use a crystal for Angel EFT. Crystals or gemstones are found in health shops and are readily available online via different sellers. If you have never used crystal before its worth reading up a bit to see which one might suit you, or else just browse in a shop and see which one 'speaks' to you. Crystals have an energy of their own and work well with angel work. I like using polished gemstones and using the touch and breathe technique just holding the crystal on the points rather than using it to tap. Remember to cleanse your crystals if you are using them. They like to be outside in the moonlight on the grass if possible, although there are many other ways to cleanse them. You can ask the angels to cleanse your crystals too.

There are books all about crystals and what their healing properties are. I have seen differences in the various books as to what you should use them for. So for me, although I like to look up what they are for, I also like to choose them intuitively. For example, if a rose quartz is meant for the heart chakra but I feel guided to use it for the throat; I will follow my guidance and use it for the throat. Crystal Angel Tapping with an Angelite crystal for Angel Signs[5]

Three deep breaths at heart centre holding the crystal to the heart centre under the hands. Then place the crystal on the tapping points as you go around the points as usual.

HC: Angels I would love to open myself up to getting angel signs

TH: Signs that really let me know you are there

TE: I really feel you are there for me

EB: But I'd love some confirmation

SE: Opening myself up to being more accessible

UE: Being aware of the ways in which you let me know you are here

UN: Thank you angels for giving me a sign today

CH: That I will easily recognise

CB: I am so grateful in advance

Th: I just love receiving confirmation that you are there

---

5   If you find you are constantly asking the angels for signs, it might be an indication that you are actually blocking them. The energy of striving, yearning and such can bring about a sense of desperation and lower your frequency. It's lovely to get angel signs, so why not write them down in a special book when you get them. Then on days when you need a boost, look over this book to reassure yourself. The angels are always there for you, and assist you when you ask. They do not need to keep showing you white feathers, angel shaped clouds, music, fragrance as a way of proving themselves. When you really welcome them into your life you will not keep requesting signs, as you are confident that they are there, and you are in a higher frequency which helps life flow better.

If: Opening myself up and releasing anything that may have been holding me back

Mf: I am so grateful to connect with my angels

Rf: Things run so much more smoothly in my life when I feel this connection

Bf: Thank you for hearing me, angels

KC: Thank you for being there

Three deep breaths at heart centre

HC: I am open to getting an angel sign today

Consider how you might continue after this round; what else do you need/want?

<u>Clearing a Space, getting ready for healing</u>

It is from my reiki and angel training that I learned the importance of clearing a space for healing work. You can do this thoroughly, taking your time, using various rituals and ensuring everything is lovely, or you can do it quickly in your mind, asking the angels and St Germain. St Germain is an Ascended Master associated with the Violet Flame of transmutation, a great energy to call upon for clearing and purifying things. *It is not essential to clear a space each time you do Energy EFT.* To do so might make what is meant to be simple and always accessible become complicated and cumbersome. You can tap any place, any time. However, if you want to do something a bit special, such as clearing something that's really deep and long-standing for you or for a client, it can be a good idea to clear the space.

Why clear a space? Sometimes rooms hold the energy of other people or things that have gone on or been in there. Thought forms etc can hang around. It doesn't take a moment to call upon Archangel Zadkiel and St Germain, or an angel of your choice. When I have finished working with clients I will always call upon them to clear me and the room I was working in and often beforehand as well. It's now as quick as a thought in my head and a deep breath. But if a place needs more thorough clearing, you can do any of the following or your own preferred variation:

● Light a candle, tap on St Germain/ the Violet Flame/Archangel Zadkiel for clear, beautiful energy for the room.

● Use sage or smudge sticks, which you light and then waft the smoke around with the intention of clearing the energy. Some people also use a large feather doing this to waft the smoke, Native American style.

● Light incense or joss stick and do as above, wafting it in all the corners of the room. If you have reiki symbols or use other symbols for healing, you can 'draw' the symbols with your incense.

● Chant or play a recorded version of a mantra for several minutes for as long as feasible. There are many, many mantras that would be suitable, you should use what resonates, I love the Gayatri mantra or Om, Om Mani Padme Hum or Om Namah Shivaya.

● Proxy tap in a mantra for the room, see Chapter 10 for proxy tapping instructions.

● Tap on love for the room. Love is very powerful and clears away fear.

● Play an angel visualisation, you don't need to stay with it, you can just allow it to play itself in the room.

● Call in the angels of the building or area to clear the room and visualise them transmuting any fear into beautiful light energy.

Grounding after Angel EFT

As with any meditative or angel work, and sometimes Energy EFT, it is important to check in to see if we or our Energy EFT partner or client is grounded. So that when they go off and do whatever it is they need to do next they are okay to do that, focused etc. How to recognise if you or someone else is ungrounded:

- Feeling or looking spaced out or woozy

- Feeling outside of your body

- Seeing into other realms after meditation has finished in a way that is distracting to what's actually happening in this realm (some people are quite psychic and that's fine but if they keep seeing or sensing things that is unhelpful this can be a sign of being ungrounded)

- Giddiness

- Excessive talking without really thinking or being aware of the recipient

How to deal with being ungrounded:

Techniques to ground someone:

- Observing rules of touch and checking with them first, place your hands on their shoulders (this opens up the chakras in the soles of the feet which has a grounding effect). Alternatively ask them to visualise their angel or spirit guide placing hands on their shoulders and explain that this opens up the chakras in the feet to ground them

- Give them a glass of water to drink slowly and mindfully

- Give them Rescue Remedy[6]

- Get them to walk around in bare feet, outside is preferable on the earth

- Drumming

---

6   Rescue Remedy (trademark) is a Bach Flower remedy combination, available in drops, spray or lozenges and contains an equal amount each of rock rose, impatiens, clematis, star of Bethlehem and cherry plum remedies, and is best known for its calming effect in times of stress and worry.

- Food

- Rest

- Visualise roots growing down from the soles of their feet going deep into the earth, connecting with the heart of the earth

- Imagine being a tree

- Foods particularly good for grounding are root vegetables, but any food is good if these are not available

If you are working with someone who becomes ungrounded ask them if this happens to them in other circumstances or if it's happened before. For some people this may never have happened before and it's good to de-brief them about it. If it happens a lot you could work on techniques with them that could help. There are also yoga asanas and mudras that help with grounding, and crystal gem stones (incl. hematite, tourmaline).

On one occasion I saw a client become suddenly ungrounded after doing classical EFT for the first time. I helped her to ground herself by visualising roots and drinking a glass of water. Its good practise to be aware of how to spot either being ungrounded yourself, or in other people and what steps to take.

Chapter Summary:

● Visualising with the angels prior to tapping connects us to the angels in preparation for tapping and can give us insights about what we should be tapping on.

● Visualising with the angels after tapping can anchor new concepts and deepen the insights we get from tapping.

● Tapping on the name of an angel or group of angels is a very effective and straightforward way to bring the angels into our Energy EFT practise.

● We can address the angels in our Energy EFT round - talking to them as we tap.

● Visualising the angels tapping with us, either tapping beside us or lighting up the meridian points as we tap is another powerful visualisation strategy in Angel EFT.

● You can ask the angels to supercharge your hands with the colour gold to enhance your tapping experience.

● If you use prayer, you can tap whilst you pray.

● Angel cards complement Energy EFT and can be used prior to or after a tapping round to enhance insights.

● Crystals or gemstones work well in Angel EFT and you can hold the stone on each tapping point instead of tapping.

● It is good to know about how to clear a space for healing, but also that if in doubt, its fine to just tap.

● It's helpful to be able to recognise in yourself and in others when a person is ungrounded and strategies to get grounded again.

● The Aspects Model helps us to work with past or future aspects of ourselves or our clients by referring to these parts as aspects which gives us more conscious control over our experiences.

Chapter 4: Archangels

Archangels are like angel managers, ever-so-nice managers of course. They can direct other angels. The Archangels are omnipresent, so if you call upon Archangel Michael and 17,000 other people are doing so at the same time, he can help everyone simultaneously. Whilst there are millions of Archangels, there are only a small portion connecting with us here on earth at this time, but the number has increased in recent years. I have included here some of the Archangels that are working here on Earth at the moment, and some ways in which you can work with them including some Angel EFT tapping scripts. The list here is by no means exhaustive. There are so many ways in which you could choose to work with any one Archangel. If you feel inspired to work with one for something different, follow that.

I learned about the Archangels primarily from the work of Diana Cooper and of Doreen Virtue.

Archangel Ariel means lion or lioness of God, helps with manifesting things, releasing spirits, protection of nature, the elementals and water bodies. You can call upon Archangel Ariel for help with nature, and to guide you in how to assist the planet and nature causes, also for abundance and manifesting things. Ariel can help you in the great outdoors, camping and the like. She is connected to the elementals and faery communities.

Angel EFT example for working with Archangel Ariel for helping Mother Earth

Three deep breaths at heart centre
HC: Archangel Ariel I call upon you now to guide me in how to help the planet
TH: I have a deep love of nature and want to do anything I can to help

TE: I am open to your guidance in how best to do this

EB: I am happy to serve and help in whatever way is helpful

SE: And to help raise the consciousness of my fellow humans so they can assist too

UE: I let go of fear based thinking around nature now

UN: So that I can simply be proactive and help things to move forward

CH: Thank you Archangel Ariel for your guidance and prompts

CB: I am happy to serve nature and to help others to do the same

Th: I breathe in the energy of Mother Earth into my being

If: And I feel refreshed and inspired and ready to act

Mf: Healing for nature

Rf: Setting a good example for others in loving our planet

Bf: Thank you Archangel Ariel for your guidance and love

KC: Thank you for being by my side

HC: Serving nature now with dedication and love

What else might Mother Earth need? Do a very simplified Positive EFT round on a quality you would wish for Mother Earth, finishing up with Thank you Archangel Ariel. Keep going!

Archangel Azrael helps out with the dying, the bereaved and newly crossed over souls. People who deal with others who are bereaved such as counsellors or simply friends of those who are bereaved can call upon Archangel Azrael to help out.

Angel EFT example for working with Archangel Azrael for helping others who are bereaved

Three deep breaths at heart centre

HC: Archangel Azrael please help me to support others who are bereaved

TH: I can see the pain they are in and I really feel for them

TE: I want my energy to be pure and clear so that I may help

EB: And I am open to your guidance

SE: Please guide me in saying the right things

UE: So that I can help in any way I can

UN: And to know when its okay to be silent

CH: To be a good listener

CB: And to protect my own energy

Th: Around people who are feeling great sadness

If: I wish to be comforting and supportive

Mf: Thank you Archangel Azrael for your wisdom and guidance

Rf: It's not down to me to take people's pain away

Bf: Help me to be accepting of other people's human experiences

KC: Whilst being a good support and minding my own energy

HC: Thank you Archangel Azrael for your loving assistance

Think of simplified rounds you could follow up with using a positive word such as 'comfort,' 'intuition,' or suchlike, finishing at HC with 'thank you Archangel Azrael.'

Nb) This can also be done as a proxy tapping approach. See also Chapter 8 healing the heart chakra in bereavement with Archangel Chamuel

Archangel Butyalil works to show us our brilliance as intergalactic beings. He works alongside Archangel Metatron in coordinating the flow of the universes. He is directing a lot of energy to Earth at the moment because of the huge shift of consciousness from third to fifth dimension which is currently unfolding. His energy spreads through water and you can connect with him best whilst being in contact with water (bathing, showering, being at the ocean etc), this way he can charge our cells with his mighty energy.

Angel EFT example for connecting with Archangel Butyalil (do this in contact with or near water)

Three deep breaths at heart centre

HC: Archangel Butyalil I call upon you now to light up my cells

TH: I receive your pure white light now

TE: *No talking just breathe comfortable full breath as you feel the energy integrate*

EB: *No talking just breathe comfortable full breath*

SE: Thank you for your assistance in removing the veils of amnesia

UE: I open myself up to fifth dimensional ways of being

UN: Allowing my consciousness to raise and to anchor

CH: Thank you Archangel Butyalil for your assistance on planet Earth right now

CB: *No talking just breathe comfortable full breath as you feel the energy integrate*

Th: *No talking just breathe comfortable full breath*

If: Thank you showing me the magnificent intergalactic being that I am

Mf: I choose to shine my light now

Rf: Assisting the great masters in raising the frequency of the planet

Bf: I willingly expand my light and see my role as an intergalactic being

KC: I am open to your loving guidance

HC: I acknowledge my role in the vastness of the universe

Spend some time anchoring the energy and then ground yourself and drink a glass of water.

Archangel Chamuel looks after the heart chakra and can help you find lost items. So if you want to meet a partner, or heal a relationship whether romantic or otherwise, you can call upon this Archangel for assistance. Also in bereavement or broken heartedness, and where forgiveness is required towards self or others. We hold resentment in the heart chakra and releasing this can really set us free.

Angel EFT for working with Archangel Chamuel for finding a romantic partner

Three deep breaths at heart centre

HC: Archangel Chamuel please help me to find a wonderful partner

TH: I am open to lining up my energy now to attract this

TE: I lovingly release any blocks in my heart now with your help

EB: So that I may experience romance and joy

SE: I allow any worries I may have had about this to be released now

UE: Visualising joyful me in an ideal romantic relationship

UN: Thank you for helping me to attract a great partner

CH: I am open to signs and prompts from you now

CB: I am willing to make any changes as needed in the way I do things

Th: And release any old patterns that may have been restricting me

If: Please remove any limiting symbols in my heart energy now

Mf: And replace them with ones that support my goals

Rf: So that I am free to attract a loving partner

Bf: Thank you Archangel Chamuel for your loving support

KC: Thanks in advance for my loving partner

HC: Aligning my vibration to a blissful romantic relationship now

Spend a moment to tune into how you would like to feel, deeply in love with a wonderful partner. Tap some more rounds on the qualities you would like to enjoy in your relationship, e.g. passion / understanding / love / empathy / adventure / trust etc. If any resistance comes up, make a note of it and tap on it. Finish by thanking Archangel Chamuel at HC.

Archangel Christiel is a great Universal Archangel connecting with the Christ energy and works with us in activating the causal chakra at the fifth dimension. When this chakra is open we can receive downloads of pure light and connect only with higher frequency beings of light.

For an example of tapping with Archangel Christiel see Chapter 14: Ascension Work: The Fifth Dimensional Chakras

Archangel Fhelyai supports the well-being of animals on earth and those that are in spirit. I have also included proxy tapping with Archangel Fhelyai in Chapter 10. Call upon Archangel Fhelyai to help animals that you are concerned about or to raise the consciousness of humans around how we treat animals.

Angel EFT for guiding life purpose working with animals with Archangel Fhelyai

Three deep breaths at heart centre

HC: Archangel Fhelyai please assist me in finding the perfect way to help animals

TH: I love helping animals and feel this is part of my life purpose

TE: I would like your help in being able to do this in a meaningful way

EB: Please support me in getting ideas

SE: And attracting ideal opportunities

UE: So that we may work together in helping animals

UN: I choose to be open to signs and guidance

CH: I welcome new doors to open for me now

CB: I am ready to think positive and hold my vision

Th: So that I can help lots of animals

If: Thank you Archangel Fhelyai for your loving guidance

Mf: And assistance for animals

Rf: I am open to serving in this way

Bf: Thank you for making this possible for me in a way I never thought of before

KC: In a way that supports me and my other life goals

HC: Feeling joyous as I help animals as part of my life purpose

What qualities do you wish for animals and your work with them? Tap some positives for yourself, and/or the animals and finish with 'thank you Archangel Fhelyai.'

Archangel Gabriel helps us with lots of things, including purifying our life, clarifying our next step or life purpose, writing and communicating, children/parenting/fertility/adoption. Archangel Gabriel also looks after the base, sacral and navel chakras.

Angel EFT for higher frequency parenting with Archangel Gabriel

Three deep breaths at heart centre
HC: Archangel Gabriel please assist me as a loving parent to ..... (name of child or children)
TH: I wish to raise my frequency now
TE: Please purify my energy with your diamond light
EB: And help me to enlighten the way I am as a parent
SE: At every moment I have been doing the best I can
UE: And I forgive myself for all the times I would like to have done things differently
UN: I choose to be open to your guidance and wisdom now
CH: Helping me to anchor a fifth dimensional state around my children
CB: Healing away and releasing any old parenting patterns
Th: That I had inherited and which no longer serve
If: Sending love and acceptance to my own parents and the ones before them
Mf: And stepping up my energy now
Rf: Thank you Archangel Gabriel for holding me and my children in your high frequency light
Bf: Guiding my words and decisions
KC: I choose to enhance myself as a parent in a loving way
HC: I am open to your support in high frequency parenting now

What else do you want/need as a high frequency parent to help you? Keep tapping on some more positives to raise you up the SUE Scale and anchor in your progress. Complete with 'thank you Archangel Gabriel' at HC.

Archangel Haniel is connected to the sacred feminine and the moon; you can call upon her for female matters although she doesn't work exclusively with women. Archangel Haniel helps to heal blocks in sexuality, and also women who grew up in an environment where women were put down or led to feel inferior. Developing your intuition and clairvoyance are also Archangel Haniel's speciality. You can call upon her also if you want to keep calm when you might otherwise be feeling anxious - tests, giving a talk, etc.

Angel EFT for women embracing the sacred feminine with Archangel Haniel
Close your eyes and ask the angels to bless your healing hands with their golden light. Sense the hands glowing and feeling energised by the angels.

Three deep breaths at heart centre
HC: Archangel Haniel please help me to embrace the sacred feminine
TH: I wish to tune into my Goddess energy now
TE: I lovingly release anything that has been getting in the way of this
EB: Anything I have been taught or understood that stops me from enjoying being a woman
SE: Thank you for showing me any blocks I have been experiencing
UE: So that I can work through and release them with love
UN: I celebrate my divine feminine nature now
CH: Stepping into my power
CB: Loving being a woman
Th: Sending healing and forgiveness to anyone who needs it
If: I choose to tune into the sacredness of my being
Mf: And celebrate my body in the feminine self
Rf: Thank you Archangel Haniel for blessing me with your gentle and powerful moon energy
Bf: I am open and receptive to your guidance
KC: I send love and light to every aspect of myself in this lifetime
HC: I celebrate being a woman in this body now

Spend some time at the heart centre with eyes closed, tune into any guidance or ideas you are getting to help you with this.

Archangel Jeremiel assists us in reviewing ourselves in how we are doing in life. He also helps newly passed spirits to do this, but you can do this any time. Any changes you'd like to make or to reflect on how you are doing on your journey in this life so far, can be helped with the loving spiritual supporter, Archangel Jeremiel.

Angel EFT for reviewing your life with Archangel Jeremiel
Visualise: Allow yourself to really relax, light a candle if you can. Feel your feet firmly planted on the floor and visualise roots travelling down deep into the earth. Seeing a waterfall of light flowing down from above imagine your whole body filling with light. Allow yourself even more relaxation now. Allow the light to cleanse and clear your energy field and flow easily through the meridians, lighting up your energy body. Call Archangel Jeremiel to your side now, he has a very gentle presence. Tell him about any concerns you have, things you would like to change in the way you live, seeing yourself in a compassionate light and visualising yourself doing things in the new way and feeling really good about yourself. Archangel Jeremiel lovingly supports your vision, and helps you to heal away any old patterns or behaviours that don't serve you.

Three deep breaths at heart centre
HC: Archangel Jeremiel please help me now to make the changes I'd love to see in my life
TH: I want to make the very most of my life here
TE: I want to release certain things now (you can state what these are)
EB: The way I do things some times
SE: I'd love to do differently
UE: I'm asking your support and guidance in raising my frequency around these issues now
UN: I forgive myself for any of the times I feel I could have done better
CH: I choose compassion and to receive the learning

CB: Opening my awareness
Th: I forgive anyone who modelled this for me
If: Breaking free from any unhelpful ancestral patterns now
Mf: I invite and embrace the freedom to make new patterns in my life
Rf: Which serve me and those around me
Bf: Thank you for guiding me Archangel Jeremiel
KC: For your loving support in making these changes
HC: I choose to really enjoy and make the most of my life now

Archangel Jophiel oversees the crown chakra and we can work with him to develop this. Also call upon Archangel Jophiel for cleansing our thoughts so that we think about beauty, to help our creative activities, and for spiritual mastery. Those who are studying can ask for Archangel Jophiel's help, he is also assisting teachers in schools and works with education. An Energy EFT round with Archangel Jophiel is included in Chapter 3, for bringing more beauty into the home.

Archangel Joules works with the oceans, and is associated with a deep aquamarine colour. He works with aquatic beings in cleansing and clearing the oceans, as well as helping the frequency of the water to remain high. He reminds us of the importance of blessing the water we drink, swim in and bathe in, as part of our spiritual evolution and development. His twin flame is Archangel Roquiel.

Angel EFT for blessing a glass of drinking water with Archangel Joules

Three deep breaths at heart centre
HC: Archangel Joules please bless this water
TH: So that I may take it into my body as fifth dimensional energy
TE: I accept the blessings that unfold for me as I work to raise my frequency and light levels

EB: *No talking just breathe comfortable full breath as you feel the energy integrate*

SE: *No talking just breathe comfortable full breath*

UE: Thank you for activating my fifth dimensional self through water

UN: And for helping me to remember to do this with the water that I use

CH: Blessing it and offering gratitude for it

CB: I accept your light and wisdom

Th: I am open to your guidance in both serving and benefiting from water

If: *No talking just breathe comfortable full breath as you feel the energy integrate*

Mf: *No talking just breathe comfortable full breath*

Rf: I receive the blessings from this water now

Bf: Thank you Archangel Joules

KC: For all the work you are doing with the earth's waters

HC: Thank you for this light

Archangel Mariel works with the soul star chakra (see Chapter 14) which is activated only in people who are ready for this higher energy. This chakra activates our skills and talents for the advantage of our family and for all of civilisation. The soul star chakra can be worked with when a person is fully ready to raise up to fifth dimensional living and this is explained more, as well as Angel EFT with Archangel Mariel, in Chapter 14.

Archangel Metatron is a mass creator of light and he uses sacred geometry. Sacred geometry contains sacred universal patterns which are utilised in the design of everything in our reality, and most often seen in holy architecture and art. This value system is widespread and found even in prehistoric times. Archangel Metatron has had, and continues to have a huge role in the enlightenment of our planet. Many lightworkers (people who are aware of an innate desire to bring more light to this planet and often beyond) are attuned to his energy. As well as his planetary and universal work, you can call on this Archangel to help with children who are very sensitive. Recent years have seen a huge increase in the diagnosis of children with Autism and ADHD, and similar conditions. Whilst often the diagnosis fits the bill, there is also the spiritual question of these being highly evolved, sensitive souls who find earth and lower vibrational ways in society difficult to comprehend and fit in with. At the fifth dimension Archangel Metatron oversees the activation of the stellar gateway chakra.

Angel EFT for a parent or caregiver of a child diagnosed with Autism or ADHD with Archangel Metatron

Three deep breaths at heart centre

HC: Archangel Metatron please assist me in understanding the needs of my child

TH: I am open to your guidance in how best to help them

TE: I choose to acknowledge the sensitive soul that s/he is

EB: I wish to do the best I can as their parent (or caregiver)

SE: Thank you for guiding us to the help and support that is for the highest good of …..

UE: And for helping us steer clear of things that aren't helpful

UN: Give me the courage Archangel Metatron when I find things challenging

CH: The strength to stay focused and calm

CB: I appreciate your help and support with ……..

Th: I know what a radiant soul that ………… is

If: Please help ………….. now to cope with the energies here

Mf: And for others to appreciate his/her light

Rf: I choose to stay centred in the knowing that we are loved and supported by the angels

Bf: Thank you Archangel Metatron

KC: For all the help you are giving us

HC: Thank you for this guidance and support

How might you evolve this now? What energy/quality would you wish for yourself as a parent and for your child? Use one-word positives to keep going and complete with 'thank you Archangel Metatron' at HC.

Archangel Michael is like a celebrity Archangel to me, because practically everyone I have met who loves angels knows about and loves Archangel Michael. He is the protector, the spiritual bouncer, and you can call on him to look after things that you are worried about. He also works with the throat chakra, and can help us with throat chakra issues such as assertiveness, creativity, communication and healing a sore throat for example. Archangel Michael can help bring spirits that are lingering on the earth plane to the light. In visualisations you can call upon Archangel Michael to place you in his royal blue cloak of light, or a bubble of blue light, or any other protection you can think of for your energy. He also helps us with his mighty sword of light to cut cords (see Chapter 3).

Angel EFT for working with Archangel Michael for courage around harsh or dominating people

Three deep breaths at heart centre
HC: Archangel Michael please shine courage and strength upon me now
TH: I would like to learn to speak my truth with love
TE: And to stand up for myself
EB: I sometimes feel pushed around
SE: And I get annoyed that I have allowed this to happen
UE: I thank the harsh or dominating people in my life right now
UN: For showing me this part of myself
CH: Giving me the opportunity to heal this
CB: I ask for your shield to protect me from their harshness
Th: And for you to fully activate my throat chakra so that I can easily stand up for myself
If: Allowing myself that courage now

Mf: Thank you Archangel Michael
Rf: For protecting me from harsh energies
Bf: Helping me to release any stuff I am carrying in my being around this
KC: I speak my truth with love and confidence
HC: I am loved, protected and supported wherever I go

Keep tapping using a word of your choice such as 'courage' finishing with 'thank you Archangel Michael at HC.

Archangel Purlimiek is the nature angel and you can connect in order to help nature or for wisdom that is encoded in it. Also, for people living in cities or working in places for long hours that are not in nature you can invoke Archangel Purlimiek to cleanse your energy with the spirit of nature.

Angel EFT to tune into the energy of nature with Archangel Purlimiek

Three deep breaths at heart centre
HC: Archangel Purlimiek please bring the energy of nature into my being now
TH: I wish to refresh my energy
TE: Being away from nature at the moment I would like to access it with your help
EB: I tune into the energy of the trees, oceans, flowers (*whatever you like that's in nature*)
SE: Accepting that freshness and pure energy into my being now
UE: Thank you for helping me to make more opportunities in my life
UN: To spend time in nature physically
CH: And helping me to access the beauty of nature in my meditation time
CB: I send love to those working to help Mother Nature
Th: Helping the consciousness of mankind to rise
If: So that we respect nature and cherish it

Mf: Thank you Archangel Purlimiek for the energy of nature flowing through my being

Rf: I am grounded and refreshed

Bf: I carry the spirit of nature in my being

KC: *No talking just breathe comfortable full breath as you feel the energy integrate*

HC: Tune in with eyes closed imagine your roots going down to the centre of the earth, like tree roots. Sense the energy of nature around you. Be open to insights.

Archangel Raguel helps us with our relationships and works with justice and fairness. He also helps attract new friendships and help relationships at work and home.

Case Example: Marian was feeling really unfairly treated at work. Her manager just seemed to have it in for her, she explained. She was constantly being criticised and given the worst tasks to do. We did a round for justice and fairness in the workplace that went something like this:

Three deep breaths at heart centre

HC: Archangel Raguel please help my work situation where I am feeling so unfairly treated

TH: I would like you and my angels to step in now

TE: I lovingly release anything that I am doing to attract unfair treatment

EB: I am willing to be open to any messages and guidance from my angels around this

SE: Thank you for shining your light on my relationship with ....

UE: Thank you for bringing justice and fairness to the situation

UN: I lovingly release fear from my being now with the help of my angels

CH: It's okay for me to stand up for myself

CB: And to expect to be treated fairly

Th: Please mirror ....'s actions if they continue so that they can see what they are doing

If: I opt for peace over pain

Mf: I invite justice and fairness into the situation

Rf: Thank you Archangel Raguel for assisting with this

Bf: I am open and responsive to your guidance

KC: I take the actions necessary on my part

HC: To move this forward for the highest good of all

Now think of a quality you would like to anchor in your energy, such as confidence or whatever you think you need. Keep going, and checking the SUE Scale.

There is also a tapping round in Chapter 11 for relationships with Archangel Raguel.

Archangel Raphael helps us with healing and manifesting. In charge of the third eye chakra, you can call upon Archangel Raphael for your abundance and for visualising and attracting things you want into your life. For healers this Archangel lovingly guides and assists. Call upon Archangel Raphael for safe, smooth travel. Also for people struggling with addictions he can intervene with their permission to make things easier and cut the cords attaching them to the behaviour or substance (see chapter 6).

Archangel Raziel has beautiful rainbow energy and works with knowledge helping us to become more spiritual. Releasing blocks accumulated in this lifetime and in past time, Archangel Raziel (Ratziel) is the Chokmah, or second aspect of God, Archangel.

Case Example: When John worked with this Archangel in dealing with his fearfulness of success issues, he saw an image of himself being crushed in a vice in another life time, because of his success and power. This played in his energy field as a fear of being too successful, and with Archangel Raziel he was able to heal the remnants of this fear, and move forward. More on past life issues can be found in see Chapter 7.

Archangel Roquiel works with the earth star chakra at fifth dimension and with the energy portals and Lady Gaia. See Chapter 14 for an Angel EFT exercise with Archangel Roquiel.

Archangel Sandalphon is said to be a very tall angel, reaching right up into the heavens. He who wears sandals before God, so called, delivers our prayers to Source. He also looks after the development of the earth star chakra along with Archangel Roquiel. Call on Archangel Sandalphon for help with music also, or to bring more music into your life. Another thing you can ask of this mighty Archangel is to place you in a fifth dimensional bubble of light, keeping your frequency at fifth dimension no matter where you go and who you are around. Practise this regularly for better effect.

Doing Angel EFT to energise a prayer with Archangel Sandalphon, you could visualise: *Close your eyes and ground yourself, linking into the light of Source also through the crown chakra. Think of the prayer or request you have and call Archangel Sandalphon to support you with this. Imagine he is holding out a basket in front of you and you are placing your prayers into that basket. Thank Archangel Sandalphon as he takes your prayers up to God, know that you are loved and cared for.*

Archangel Uriel works with the angels of peace and you can call upon him to direct these angels of peace anywhere you like. Also, master of the solar plexus chakra, Archangel Uriel is helping us to dissolve fear and things that have been blocking us from really stepping up to the lives our Soul came here to live. I have included solar plexus work with Archangel Uriel in Chapters 8 and 14.

Archangel Zadkiel works with Ascended Master St Germain to bring us the Violet Flame, and also the Gold, Silver and Violet Flame of transmutation.

Ascended Masters are very high frequency beings of light who were humans in past incarnations, but have gone through spiritual transformations sometimes known as initiations.

Angel EFT for clearing your energy with Archangel Zadkiel and the Violet Flame

Three deep breaths at heart centre
HC: Archangel Zadkiel please clear my energy now with the Violet Flame
TH: I release all that which does not serve
TE: From my energy now for transmutation
EB: Thank you Violet Flame for cleansing and clearing me
SE: Allowing me to easily release fear now
UE: Any of the blocks to my happiness and peace I surrender now
UN: Thank you for this clearing
CH: I invite the energy of peace and wisdom
CB: I allow my energy body health and well-being
Th: I no longer need to hold onto stale, stuck energy
If: I lovingly release these with the mighty Violet Flame
Mf: I thank you for this light
Rf: This bright light in my being
Bf: Thank you Archangel Zadkiel
KC: For overseeing this clearing of my energy now
HC: Thank you for my revitalised clear energy

 The Quick Reference Archangel Chart (overleaf) is also available as a PDF download for free at www.angeleft.com

QUICK REFERENCE ARCHANGEL CHART

Archangel	Meaning	Helps with...
Ariel	Lion or lioness of God	Manifestation, protection of nature and elementals and water bodies, spirit releasing
Azrael	Whom God helps	Bereavement and spirits crossing over after death, grief counsellors
Butyalil		Universal Angel keeps order the vast universal currents
Chamuel	He who sees God or he who seeks God	Love, heart healing, romance and relationships. Finding lost items, finding your way when you feel lost
Christiel		Develops the causal chakra, helps to silence the mind so that we can receive downloads and be at peace
Fhelyai	Pronounced 'Felyay'	Looks after the welfare of animals, both on earth and those in spirit
Gabriel	Hero of God or God is my strength	Purifying, clarity on your next step. Writing and communications. Children and child-birth, adoption
Haniel	Glory of God or Grace of God	Grace, moon energy, calm when giving talk or performances etc., healing, psychic ability and intuition
Jeremiel	Mercy of God	Life review and making life changes, dream interpretation, clairvoyance and visions
Jophiel	Beauty of God	Artistic projects and artists, creative pursuits. Beautiful thoughts, interior decorating, slowing down, crown chakra

Joules		Oceans
Mariel		Developing the higher aspect of the soul star chakra, brings energy and light from the sun
Metatron	The angel of the presence	Sacred geometry, helps Earth connect to other planets, stellar gateway chakra, ascension pathway, mass healing
Michael	One who is like God	Protection, warrior energy, cord cutting, spiritual bouncer. Spirit releasing. Patron Saint of police
Purlimiek		Nature kingdom and elementals
Raguel	Friend of God	Resolving arguments, defending the unfairly treated, empowerment, cooperation, friendships
Raphael	God has healed	Healing, assisting healers, releasing addictions, helping animals, spirit release. Manifestation, third eye
Raziel	Secret of God	Divine secrets of the Universe, alchemy, clairvoyance, manifestation, psychic abilities
Roquiel		Works with Earth Star chakra, Lady Gaia, healing the leylines and portals
Sandalphon	He who wears sandals before God	Delivering prayers to God, music, deep earth energy and earth star chakra development
Uriel	Fire of God	Solar plexus chakra, wisdom, transmuting fear, studies and tests, writing, alchemy, divine magic
Zadkiel	Righteousness of God	Violet Flame of transmutation, forgiveness, memory

Chapter Summary:

● Archangels are like supervisors to the angels, and direct them in their work as needed.

● They are omnipresent and can help many, many people simultaneously.

● Different Archangels can help with different issues, but you can feel free to call on any Archangel for anything you feel drawn to.

● The Archangels help enhance your Angel EFT as they bring in a very specific energy unique to each one.

Chapter 5: Energy Hygiene

We all have energy, whether or not we are ever interested in it or aware of it. Our energy is ever-changing. It is influenced by what is around us, although we can improve our resilience around difficult energies and learn to replenish the stocks. Our feelings and emotions affect our energy, and vice versa. Some of us take on the energy of other people. Sensitive children unconsciously try to heal their parents' energy. In the process they can end up carrying some of the unhealthy energy for the parent. Unfortunately, as unhealthy as this is it doesn't even remove any of the pain from the parent who feels even worse as they — unconsciously - know their child is doing this. This is one way that depression, shame, anxiety and so on can pass along the generations. Similarly, healthy parents pass on healthy energy. There are of course other variables involved.

What would you like your energy to be like? What qualities? It's easier to bring these about once you know what it is you want. Call to mind a time — if you aren't already - when you were feeling really happy and joyful and everything was going really well. Your energy was bright and clear and healthy at that time, radiant. Like plus 7 or above on the SUE Scale. What happens next? If we are not in a good space just now, sometimes our thoughts start telling us stories of woe, as to why we couldn't be that happy just now because.... If we are able to really tune into that good feeling and welcome that energy into our energy body now, this can lift the energy really fast.

The angels can help of course, and making sure that our focus is on gratitude rather than on things that aren't going quite how we'd like.

Three deep breaths at heart centre
HC: Angels help me to bring more joy into my energy now
TH: I invite the energy of joy

TE: I lovingly release any limiting beliefs that have been affecting my energy now

EB: Thank you angels for helping me to celebrate the blessings in my life now

SE: I don't need to take on anyone else's energy or stuff

UE: I'm doing people a favour by having really healthy joyful energy

UN: Inviting joy into every part of my being

CH: I radiate joy

CB: I love feeling joyful

Th: Angels of joy surrounding me now

If: Helping to lift my vibration and keep it raised

Mf: Thank you for the energy of joy

Rf: Which fills and permeates my being

Bf: And all that I say and do

KC: Thank you for this joy that is growing in and around me now

HC: Angels of joy

Now what? Keep going. Complete with 'thank you angels,' at HC.

Barbara Ann Brennan demonstrates in her book *Hands of Light* how energies can appear, as she sees them clairvoyantly. In the book are beautiful illustrations which show us how the energies appear for her. There are many ways in which people can see or sense energies. Most people can feel the energy of tension, such as when something frightening is happening or if people are arguing even without noticing their facial expression or hearing their words. It has a vibration. Just as joy and love do.

Energy Taking

Sometimes we drain other people's energy, and sometimes others drain us. Ever been around somebody and consistently feel drained after meeting them? Some people use the term 'energy vampires,' to describe people who affect them this way. I personally think this sounds a little judgemental, and labels the person rather than their behaviour - although it certainly creates a sense of vigilance. When you are around people that drain energy you need to either protect your energy around this person or learn to replenish your energy as it is constantly available to you to do so. Both is best. There is an endless supply of energy for us to access. So if somebody has 'taken' your energy simply call in more. I like the idea of protecting my energy in certain circumstances, but also the idea that energy flows in through and out as Silvia Hartmann suggests. We can simply call for more energy with the angels and Energy EFT if we need to. People sap energy from others generally because they have not learned to access it in a healthy way. So imagine the service we EFTers are doing the world by telling others about Energy EFT. Lessening the need for energy taking.

> *There is an inexhaustible supply of energy avaliable to us on tap from the Universe*

So the next time you hear yourself or anyone else say:

'I have no energy;'

'I'm completely zapped;'

'I'm drained,' etc…

…remind them or yourself that there is always more energy. Pardon the pun, but we simply need to tap into it. I don't mean that rest is not important, and that we can be superhuman if we tapped all day on having lots of energy - although it might be fun to try. But the things we say are powerful. If you are tired, rest a bit if you can, but listen to what you are telling yourself. Your thoughts influence your energy. And if you can't rest, ask for more energy to keep you going. It's there for you. The mind and the words we use are powerful beyond measure.

Thoughts that sap our energy:	Corresponding thoughts that invite more energy:
I am no good at this	I'd love to improve at this
I hate the way that looks	I want to get that looking better
I never have any time to do the things I need	I'd like to make more space in my schedule so I can do the things I'd love to do
Life is so exhausting	I'm allowing myself some more rest just now
Poor me	I'm so glad about....
I never have enough money	I'd like to help myself to receive ..... money
What a mess	I'd like to tidy that up and get it feeling good

Types of Energy

There are energy character types such as those who have very harsh or boisterous energy, which feels a bit like they are banging into you, so to speak. Or people who seem to be throwing darts at you. I like to protect myself around these types. People who are very negative in the way they talk can leech energy if we allow our vibration to sink down. The things they are saying act a bit like bursting a balloon or being covered by a damp cloth. Caring people can tend to allow others to take their energy. They freely give it to others because of a desire to heal other people. Even though it is possible to replenish yourself, if you are one of these folks, it's best of course to teach other people to heal their own energy. And if you can't do that, to have good boundaries around such people. Giving your energy to others is usually futile and only helps replenish them for a short time.

If you suspect someone is sending you 'bad vibes' as it were, call upon Archangel Michael to shield you from this and to help the other person deal with their difficult emotions in more honourable ways. It is likely that their thoughts won't have any effect on you unless you are also attracting this yourself, however calling upon Archangel Michael will help the situation.

Mental Illnesses and Energy

Working in mental health I was able to perceive clairvoyantly, claircognizantly and clairsentiently the different vibrational characteristics of the mental illnesses and their energies. To me depression felt like a heavy, sticky darkness that hardly moved at all. Psychosis was fast moving, creeping, darting and eerie, often with fear-based spirit attachments. Mania was enormous, like a big expansion of energy around the person, and sometimes it would be euphoric or it could be dysphoric/angry. Each time it was different but I could recognise what each one was. All of the mental illnesses were permeated with fear, even manic states where the person for all intents and purposes seems elated out of their mind. I learned to seal my energy being around these intense energy types, to the point where I became less aware of them unless it was necessary. I have found being clair *anything* can be tiring if you have it switched on all of the time.

You will notice different times in your life, or even today, where your energy has felt different.

How is your energy now? Just for a moment tune in and close your eyes. Ask your energy how it is. Try not to get caught up in the story of thought, such as 'I'd have more energy if this...or that.' Instead draw upon the wisdom of the body. What does it need, if anything, to improve? It's good to be energy aware; you can help yourself easily if you need to clean up your energy.

Our energy quality changes according to what's going on for us. Sensitive people pick up on other people's sadness, anger or helplessness. They do this often without even realising, and can wonder why they are feeling that way. Even the energy of places or buildings. Old buildings can have old energy attachments, some are spirits that haven't moved on, and some are just energy. If we are sensitive we can be like sponges, absorbing all the energies, trying to help without even thinking about it. Our diet and the things we put in our body affect our energy. Drinking too much alcohol or taking drugs for example leaves the aura unsealed and messy, and we can attract all sorts of unpleasant energies and 'cling-ons.' Good energy hygiene can be protecting your energy when you need to, or even consistently each day. The other thing is to allow the flow of energy to take care of itself, in through and out. In other words letting those other energies into your own energy space but simultaneously allowing it to flow out again.

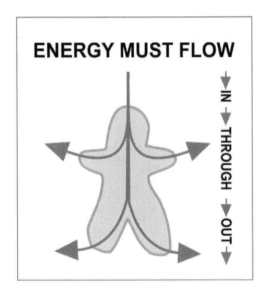

Image courtesy of 'Energy EFT' by Silvia Hartmann

It's nice to think that no matter what you have absorbed it can simply flow out again. And with this in mind if you decide to protect your energies don't think of blocking them as such, but just protecting yourself from the toxins. If your energy is in an unhealthy state it's because there are blockages - the undesirable energy that has flowed in gets stuck and you don't feel good. Energy EFT unblocks, so that the energy can flow again.

Clean up your aura with Archangel Michael and Archangel Gabriel

Your aura is an electromagnetic field around you and reflects what is going on in the energy body. In good health it is roughly shaped like an egg around your body. It has colours which can change. Some people can see auras and they can also be photographed by Kirlian photography.

Do a round using your own words according to what you want for yourself in your life, starting with 'Archangel Michael and Archangel Gabriel please assist me now in cleaning my aura'. Tap through asking first for Archangel Michael to clear away any negative energy you have in your aura, ask him to transmute it into light. Then ask Archangel Gabriel to place in your aura golden symbols of what you want to achieve in your life and things you'd like for yourself. You may be very clear about what you want in which case you can ask Archangel Gabriel to place these symbols into your aura, and so help you to attract them into physical being. Be sure to always say as well 'if these things are for my highest good', or 'this or better please.' If you are not sure about your life purpose or what you really want, ask Archangel Gabriel to light up the symbols that are already in your aura regarding your life's purpose so that the right opportunities will come your way and you will become clearer.

Visualisation:

Close your eyes and feel your feet flat on the floor. Send thick golden roots from your feet into the ground below your feet. Through the floor, through the foundation of the building if you are indoors, through the earth below. Growing deeper and deeper and down towards a great crystal at the centre of the earth. Wrap your roots right around this crystal and allow them to dip into it. Light and love flows from the great crystal back up your roots and all the way back into your physical body. Allow the light to flow through the body, lighting up every cell.

Feel yourself relaxing more deeply as this light fills and permeates throughout your being. Then notice that from above your head flows a stream of golden and white light. This fills up the energy bodies flowing in through the crown chakra and travelling around all the energy systems. Call in Archangel Michael now, ask him to scan your aura. Ask him to remove any dark patches, entities or implants now. He may do this with a type of vacuum, or with his sword of light, or by another method. Watch him clearing them away out of your aura and transmuting them into love and light. Take some deep breaths while this is happening. Make a note of any information you receive at this time.

Now call Archangel Gabriel forward and ask that he places within your aura golden symbols of that which you would like to attract, accomplish or receive. Or if you are unsure ask him to light up the symbols which are already in your aura about your life's purpose. Notice what these might be. Spend some time here. When you are ready remember your roots that you sent down, keeping you very grounded. Pull your aura in towards the body to a level that is comfortable. Thank the angels and Archangel Michael and Archangel Gabriel. Bring your awareness back into the room. Note down anything you learned from the experience.

Protect and Seal Your Aura with Archangel Michael and Archangel Metatron

Remember that you can work with any of the Archangels as you are guided, so the examples I give here are just that... examples.

Three deep breaths at heart centre
HC: Archangel Michael and Archangel Metatron please assist me in protecting and sealing my aura now
TH: Please place your blue protective light around me now Archangel Michael
TE: Sealing the edge of my aura and keeping it vibrant and healthy
EB: Archangel Metatron please place high frequency sacred geometry symbols on the outer layer of my aura now
SE: So that only high frequency energies are allowed to permeate
UE: I enjoy feeling safe and protected in my energy
UN: It benefits others when my aura is sealed

CH: I release any old beliefs that have held me back in terms of minding my energy now
CB: Any old programs that said I should take on the pain of other people
Th: I am open to learning new ways of helping myself and others
If: Which I can do without compromising my energy in any way
Mf: I love feeling safe and protected in my energy
Rf: Thank you Archangel Michael for your loving guidance and assistance
Bf: Thank you Archangel Metatron for your loving guidance and assistance
KC: I love helping others in a way that's healthy for all concerned
HC: Thank you angels for my perfectly sealed and protected aura

Close your eyes and tune in again, just visualising the two Archangels sealing your aura, and be aware of any guidance and messages.

Chapter Summary:

- Everyone has energy whether or not they ever acknowledge it.

- Energy is ever changing.

- Our feelings, thoughts and emotions affect our energy, and vice versa.

- Sensitive people take on the energy of others in an attempt to heal them and in empathy.

- Taking on the energy of others is not healthy and does not heal them.

- The things we focus our thoughts on affect our energy, and we can learn to think more energy-enhancing thoughts.

- Angels can help us to improve our energy by asking them and by doing Angel EFT.

- You can ask Archangel Gabriel to place or light up the symbols of your life's purpose in your aura or the things you'd like to attract, if they are for your highest good.

- Some people can see or sense energies. It is likely that most people can do either of these but that many people are not aware that they can do it.

- Some people drain the energy of others because they have not yet learned an effective way to access more energy by themselves.

- Your aura is an electromagnetic field around your body and reflects what is going on in the energy body.

- A technique you can use around difficult energies is to ask the angels to shield or protect you.

- You can work with the angels to clean, protect and seal your aura, including with Archangel Michael and Archangel Metatron.

- Energy flows in, through and out of the healthy energy body, so even if you have been around difficult energy and you feel you have absorbed it you can allow it to simply flow out again.

Chapter 6: Healing Unhealthy Patterns and Addictions

As a human being it is likely that everyone has had at least some self-destructive behaviours, or have experienced these before healing them and evolving out of them. Current self-destructive behaviours, whatever they may be, have been serving us up to now. We have a lower self or ego, which operates at the level of fear and drama. And we have a higher self. Our higher self always knows what is right for us and for the greater good, rather like the angels. The two step in at different times for most humans. When we operate from ego we are stressed out, and we can sabotage and make things harder on ourselves. We go against the natural flow of the universe, we don't feel worthy of going with the flow, or can't see how to do it. This is because we don't feel deserving of better, and often we are totally unaware we are doing this.

Our self-destructive patterns and addictions can be the cause and the result of difficult emotions, and often result in a vicious cycle.

A few examples of the millions of possible behaviour patterns which don't serve us:

- Arguing and criticising others
- Can't be present, always on the phone, tablet, laptop etc
- Binge drinking
- Over eating
- Addictions
- Not getting enough physical activity
- Cluttering and mess

- Paranoia or thinking people see the worst in you

- Negative self-talk, 'self-battering'

- Procrastinating and putting things off

- Watching horror films or disturbing programs, videos, literature

- Gossiping and putting others down

- Doom and gloom talk

- Perfectionism, which leads to procrastination, which gets you stuck and not taking any action

- Consistently choosing partners that end up hurting you

Case Example: Celine noticed a pattern in her energy levels as she became more accustomed to using Energy EFT and watching changes in her moods and energy. She had made major positive changes in her life over the past three years and was very self-aware. Every few days, sometimes once, sometimes twice a week, she would go from feeling good the previous day to waking up at a minus 4 and feeling uninspired to help herself. Her thoughts were negative and self-depreciating; she would then turn to eating lots of junk food throughout the day when she felt this way. She ate healthily most of the time, but binged when she felt like this, and then felt bad about herself afterwards and uncomfortable. Because she was so self-aware, she felt even more determined to overcome the behaviour of using food to try to change her mood. Especially since she was well used to the goodness that Energy EFT brought. She disliked the behaviour pattern, and it was also interfering with her desire to be slimmer.

When I asked her to describe the feeling she would get in her body on these days she said it was like a dark slimy slug in her stomach. After de-stressing we tapped on dark slimy slug which made her laugh and brought her SUE rating from a -1 up to zero. At this point we brought in Archangel Raphael and Gabriel and did a round on self-love, releasing addictions and bringing in a sense of purity. She saw the 'slug' transmuting into a star that needed her attention sometimes. She herself devised a round of Angel EFT that she used as a preventative, first thing in the morning to set the day up right. She did this for

30 days with good effect and then continued to repeat it occasionally if she felt the need:

HC: Angels please help to keep my outlook as positive as possible
TH: I choose to focus on the things I am grateful for
TE: And I know I have come a long way
EB: I release any anxiety to be transmuted by the light now
SE: I choose to release all fear from my being
UE: I am loved and I radiate love
UN: Thank you for loving me, angels
CH: Thank you for this day
CB: I love to be at my best
Th: Thank you Archangel Raphael for helping me break free from binge eating
If: I love being able to soothe my emotions in healthy ways
Mf: Thank you Archangel Gabriel for helping to purify my being
Rf: I love feeling so clear and inspired
Bf: Inspired about feeling good
KC: Allowing this good feeling to spread out through my energy now
HC: Thank you Angels for this wonderful day

She would then tap on specific qualities she wanted to experience that day, using Positive EFT and finishing with 'thank you angels.' Afterwards she would tune in for a few moments and see if the angels had any specific guidance for the day.

Work to release unhealthy patterns and addictions

If you have an unhealthy pattern you would like to let go of, give it a little thought now. It may be useful to get pen and paper and write down some things.

If you are resistive to committing, tap on this first...

Three deep breaths at heart centre

HC: Angels I feel afraid of dealing with this

TH: But here I am reading this chapter anyway

TE: A part of me wants to do some work on this and a part of me is really afraid

EB: I am choosing to really be gentle with myself and only take action when it's right for me

SE: It's okay for me to consider change today without taking any action right now

UE: I can sow a seed

UN: It's okay for me just to sow a seed today

CH: I ask for your support and guidance with this issue

CB: I am open to your loving care

Th: I am also open to some help coming my way

If: I really want to feel safe

Mf: And I promise to help myself to feel safe right now in any way I can

Rf: Even if I'm reading this chapter

Bf: I don't have to fully take on this problem today

KC: I deeply love and accept all parts of me now

HC: Thank you Angels for keeping me safe and loved

Think now of what you need and tap on that word, doing as many rounds as you need to feel much better and more confident. Finish with 'thank you angels' at HC.

Please note: for problems that feel too big to tackle on your own, please get help. Addictions, for example, usually need input from others who can see your blind spots, and that are experts in the field.

Look at the SUE Scale again. Where are you right now on the scale? What would it take for you to move up just by one? And by two?

Feeling Bad »————→ Feeling Nothing »————→ Feeling Great!

Questions to ask yourself about this issue

Try answering these questions as honestly as you can. The more you put into this work, the more you get out. Long-standing problems need consistency and repetition to clear them, it is unlikely to clear them completely first go:

- What is the unhealthy behaviour or pattern?

- What is your role in it?

- What is anyone else's role in it (e.g. who else does this too who you may feel influenced by, etc)?

- If you had a magic wand and could remove this problem entirely right now and how safe would you feel?

- If not 100% safe, why might that be?

- What's in it for you to keep up this pattern or behaviour (how is it serving you)?

- What could block you from succeeding and maintaining success in break-ing the pattern or behaviour?

- What would you like to use the newfound energy doing, which you have been using on this problem?

- What is a realistic time frame for completely overcoming this problem?

- Write down the pros and cons of this pattern/behaviour and the pros and cons of giving it up

95

- If this problem were to light up as a symbol or shape in your energy what would it look/feel like, where would it be? Draw, sketch it on your page.
- If this had a voice what would it say to you? What does it want?

Now that you have more information, call in the angels to help with this work. I recommend doing the following visualisation:

For Addictions (the long version) If you are serious about making the change for good, why not commit to practising this for 30 consecutive days?...

Clear the energy of the space you are working in. Light, or visualise a candle. Call in your angels and I like to call in the following trio of Archangels: Raphael to heal and help dissolve attachments to this behaviour or pattern, Zadkiel for the Violet Flame to clear away any fear based energy the addiction has been lingering in and Gabriel for clarity and to purify your energy.

Close your eyes and see yourself being bathed in golden light from above. Send down roots from the soles of your feet deep into the earth for grounding. See Archangel Raphael working on your energy body now, tune into the symbol or shape in your energy that the addiction represents, and allow Raphael to clear this with his powerful emerald healing light. He safely removes the symbol or energy replacing it with healing light. We often hold addictions in our sacral chakra region but be open to what your energy is telling you. Spend some time here and be aware of what you see or sense.

Now see Archangel Zadkiel bathing the site in your aura where the addictive symbol was and flooding it with the Violet Flame of transmutation. Ask him to then place a symbol of something beautiful that you would like in your aura there instead. If you can't think of anything just ask for more light to be placed there, or even a beautiful heart to symbolise love and fulfilment. Then see Archangel Gabriel placing a crown of white light on your head, giving you complete clarity around this matter, be aware of new insights. See Gabriel then placing a beam of white light through and over your whole body and auric field, purifying your energy and raising your vibration. Be aware of any sensations or new knowing. Stay in this space as long as you need to and write down any new understanding.

Now tap on these things or your own version that feels right for you:
Thank you Archangel Raphael for removing this symbol for me and for your healing energy
Thank you Archangel Zadkiel for bringing the Violet Flame
Transmuting the fear in my energy into love and more light
Thank you Archangel Gabriel for ongoing clarity around this matter
May I always be self-aware
Thank you for this new purity in my energy now
I allow it to settle in my being
I allow it to grow into other areas of my life
I know I can call upon any of you whenever I need to
I am raising my awareness to a new level now
I am giving myself permission to move forward with love now

And if appropriate you may add in:
I no longer require my old addiction
It no longer serves me as I have newfound insights now
I have access to your help whenever I need it
I send love and this knowing to my future aspects
Which may feel triggered by old triggers
I send him/her the light they need to overcome cravings

And finish with:
I offer myself now and all of my past aspects love and compassion
I deeply love, honour and forgive myself
And anyone else who may have contributed to any pain I have experienced
Thank you Archangel Raphael for being there when I need you
Thank you Archangel Gabriel for the purity and clarity of mind
Thank you Archangel Zadkiel for bringing the Violet Flame
Transmuting fear into love in my being and beyond

Now use use a further very positive round after this using a word that really excites you or makes you feel charged up for great experiences. Think of something really great that you would have the energy for or time for if you didn't have the addiction any more. Examples could include: creativity, holidays, self-love, time with family, gorgeous home, new hobby, fitness, meditation etc.

If the thought of doing the above leaves you feeling overwhelmed, remember...

"You don't need to solve it, just to evolve it."

- Silvia Hartmann

Taking the first Step

Three deep breaths at heart centre
HC: Archangel Raphael assist me now in taking the first step
TH: In helping myself with this issue
TE: I would like to take positive action today but I feel overwhelmed
EB: I want to help myself to move forward
SE: Help me now to feel calm and confident
UE: Thank you Archangel Zadkiel for cleansing my energy with the Violet Flame
UN: *No talking just deep cleansing breath*
CH: *No talking just deep cleansing breath*
CB: Thank you Archangel Gabriel for purifying my mind and my energy now
Th: *No talking just deep cleansing breath*
If: *No talking just deep cleansing breath*
Mf: I give myself permission now to progress
Rf: I am safe and loved by my angels
Bf: I choose to be calm and allow peace to flow through my body
KC: I am deeply calm and relaxed
HC: Thank you Angels for keeping me safe and loved

Other things you might like to tap on for a shorter version:

Angels I'm afraid of looking at this
I don't know what's going to come up
Don't know if I can handle it
If I let go of this addiction I wonder what I'd find
What if something else were lurking around the corner?
But I do really want to feel more in control around this
So I'm asking your help now
Help me to do this at my own pace in a way that's really safe for me
More self-control
More peace and relaxation
Healthier ways of managing stress
Healthier ways of nurturing myself becoming obvious to me now
Healthy calm me
More self-control
No need to rush it
Calm safe me

You could use a round of 'calm' or 'peace' when you are approaching the usual time you might engage in the addictive behaviour. Become curious about what triggers it, or what you associate it with. Think stress reduction. More peace, more calm, more empowered.

Tapping round for overeating with Archangels Raphael and Gabriel:

HC: Archangel Raphael please assist me in clearing away any addictions or unhealthy patterns with food now
HC: I choose to release these now

HC: I can eat light healthy foods that raise my vibration and help me to feel good

TH: Archangel Gabriel please help to purify my physical body

TE: So that each cell is bathed in your purifying light

EB: I send healing and love to every cell in my body

SE: And compassion to myself

UE: I love to feel good in my body

UN: And I am willing to work on this now

CH: Thank you angels for guiding me in my food choices

CB: I am open to being drawn to foods that are good for my body

Th: Thank you Archangel Raphael for helping me to be easily release and breathe through any cravings

If: I am allowing myself to release cravings in new ways I never thought of before

Mf: I welcome the feeling of purity in my body from eating healthy foods

Rf: Thank you Archangel Gabriel for guiding me towards healthy high vibrational foods

Bf: Sending myself love and compassion in this moment

KC: I accept love and compassion

HC: I invite love and blessings into the foods that I eat today

Close your eyes and tune in; make a note of any knowing or new insights, you may need to go on from here into another round with what came up. If you really want to heal your eating pattern, do this every day for thirty days and beyond if you need to. Where you place your focus is where you will reap the rewards.

Other Unhealthy Patterns

Case Example: Maggie had a habit of constantly putting herself down. She did it in her head with her thoughts and she did it in conversation. 'I'm so useless at this... I'm always failing at that... I'd never be able to do that; I wouldn't have the brains.' etc etc. She had a good sense of humour, which was one thing she liked about herself, but she was always the butt of her own jokes. It was something she had learned to do as an adolescent in secondary school, as a type of defence and to amuse her friends. But it carried on for decades after.

The subconscious mind is always listening and so is the universe. And so Maggie's experience matched what she said perfectly, and she often experienced what she perceived as failure, not being good at things and not having the intelligence to succeed at things. Then, at least, she could say 'I told you so, I told you I wouldn't be good at it.' So in a way, there was something in it for her to keep doing this. But there was something that really bothered her that brought her to trying out Energy EFT. She would love to learn to drive but had never permitted herself to take the test even though she had had a lot of lessons. She really loved her freedom and would love to be able to just get into a car and just drive away on an adventure. But every time someone suggested she go for the test she would reply with a barrage of reasons as to why she couldn't possibly take the test.

On our first session Maggie released a lot of tears and came to realise that there was a lot of sadness and resentment towards her father who always put girls and women down, favouring her three brothers over her and constantly encouraging them, to the neglect of her. She was shocked that this came up, as she had never remembered it until then. It had just got swept under the carpet. We worked with Archangel Chamuel for the heart chakra and forgiveness.

Maggie was angry that her father had held her back so much, and while she was not conscious of it all, this anger was being directed at herself. But now things were making sense and she was even more motivated to overcome her negative self-talk and give herself permission to do well and to follow her dreams. We did some work with the aspect of Maggie as a child experiencing all that negativity towards women and girls, working with Archangel Raguel who defends the unfairly treated. In each session to resume focus and not get side-tracked by the things coming up, we would always end with a positive round on Maggie seeing herself having passed her driving test, going off on an adventure. She would tap as though she were actually the future aspect, celebrating her success. It went like this:

HC: I am so happy and thankful that I have passed my driving test

HC: And I am starting out on an adventure

HC: All these roads to explore all by myself

TH: All this freedom

TE: I feel so free and light

EB: I love feeling so free and confident in myself

SE: I am so proud of myself for passing the test

UE: Thank you angels for all of your help

UN: And for making this an extra magical adventure today

CH: I love exploring places by myself

CB: Thank you Archangel Chamuel for helping me to find my way

Th: Thank you Archangel Ariel for helping me to create this adventure in my life

If: I am so happy and excited

Mf: I am so grateful that I could do it

Rf: Loving every minute of this journey

Bf: Excited and grateful

KC: Thank you for my confidence and self-belief

HC: I am so happy and thankful that I have passed my driving test

And sure enough, Maggie made it a reality. She passed her test first time, and she stopped putting herself down and making fun of herself, and was free to go on her driving adventures.

<u>Tapping for cluttering and mess in the home where hoarding is a problem</u>

HC: Archangel Jophiel please help me to make my home a beautiful and tranquil place

HC: Archangel Michael I ask that you clear any lower energies from my home now and help me to clear the physical space

HC: I have this tendency to be untidy and to hoard things

TH: A part of me feels threatened by throwing things away

TE: In case I need them or in case it upsets anyone

EB: The mess is really upsetting me and holding me back

SE: I'd love a clear, tidy and beautiful home space

UE: But for some reason it's been hard for me to make it happen

UN: I release now anything in my energy body that is mirroring the clutter in my home

CH: With the help of my angels I'm letting it go

CB: I don't have to clear it all at once

Th: I can take it one corner at a time

If: So that in a months' time there are amazing changes

Mf: I am free to give myself the gift of a tidy and beautiful clear home

Rf: Working on it a little each day

Bf: In a way that feels safe for me

KC: Thank you for your loving assistance Archangel Jophiel and Archangel Michael

HC: Thank you for my wonderful tranquil home

Visualise: your home as best you can, looking beautiful and clear. Hold this vision, make it as detailed as you can. If at first it's hard, re-visit it often. Be open to expanding your vision and making it more and more wonderful. Look at home styling magazines or browse around home decor shops to feed your vision.

Now tap some more positive rounds, finishing with 'thanks you angels' at HC.

 Compulsive hoarders are experiencing high levels of emotional 'noise' with the clutter, and it may be best to tackle this with an experienced practitioner, depending on the level of severity.

Tapping to overcome the destructiveness of perfectionism

HC: Archangel Jeremial please help me to make positive changes in my way of being

HC: Clearing away perfectionist traits that have been holding me back

HC: A part of me thinks it's important to be perfect

TH: And yet another part of me knows I am only human

TE: And even though I love to do things really well

EB: It's not reasonable that I must be perfect all of the time

SE: In fact, this puts me under a lot of pressure

UE: And sometimes stops me from taking any action at all

UN: I'd like to take a more balanced approach to the things I need to do in life

CH: I don't mind doing my best whenever I can

CB: And I'd really like to learn to stop and celebrate when I'm doing well

Th: Instead of landing myself with more and more challenges

If: I am going to remember to stop and enjoy the view

Mf: And be grateful for my achievements

Rf: Releasing the need to be perfect

Bf: So that I can be my very best and enjoy being that

KC: Thank you for your loving assistance Archangel Jeremial

Tune in and see what you would like more of to bring you higher on the SUE Scale just now. Keep tapping.

Clearing mild paranoia or thinking people see the worst in us

HC: Archangel Uriel please help me to release unhelpful thoughts about people seeing the worst in me

HC: Sometimes I find myself getting paranoid

HC: I'm just trying to keep safe

TH: Maybe I'm worried I'll be let down by people

TE: But thinking this all the time isn't working well for me

EB: Unhelpful thinking is really holding me back

SE: I'd love to feel more confident

UE: It's true that we can't make everyone like us

UN: But dwelling on this really brings my energy down

CH: I'd love to feel confident and self-assured

CB: I'd love to really believe in myself

Th: Not worrying about what other people think all the time

If: I am tuning into my own self confidence now

Mf: Allowing myself to really shine and be who I am

Rf: Focusing my thoughts on really being glad to be me

Bf: Nurturing and appreciating myself now

KC: Thank you for your loving assistance Archangel Uriel

Clearing arguments and criticising others (includes for parents)

HC: Archangel Raguel please work with me in improving the way I relate to people

HC: I have this habit of criticising others

HC: And it doesn't feel good

TH: I get into arguments

TE: And end up feeling worse afterwards

EB: I'd love to change this pattern

SE: I'd like to speak more kindly to other people

UE: I'd like more peace in my life

UN: So I lovingly release the need to criticise now
CH: Wherever it might come from
CB: If it was modelled for me
Th: The buck stops here
If: I am choosing words and ways of peace now
Mf: Allowing myself to love and be loved
Rf: Seeing the good in myself as well as others
Bf: Smoothing my relationships
KC: Thank you for helping me to make these changes Archangel Raguel

Visualise Archangel Michael placing a heart shape in your throat chakra which will help all of your communications to be more loving. Now imagine Archangel Raguel and Chamuel filling your aura with a rose pink colour, bringing you more love.

Keep tapping for positives. What do you need to move even higher up the SUE Scale?

Tapping about another person who does a lot of doom and gloom talk

HC: Archangels Michael and Sandalphon please help .... with their negative talk
HC: It really upsets me to have to listen to it
HC: Here am I, trying my best to be positive
TH: And listening to them can really bring me down
TE: I'd love to be shielded from that
EB: I know it's up to them
SE: I can only change the way I respond to it
UE: So maybe it's a life lesson for me
UN: But if you can help by making an opening for them

CH: To become more positive
CB: Surround them in blessings and light
Th: And I choose to help in whatever way I can
If: I choose not to subscribe to fear, even if they are talking in that way
Mf: Allowing myself to remain in a calm and positive state
Rf: And refusing to collude in their fear talk
Bf: Archangel Michael please guide me in using the right words
KC: Archangel Sandalphon please surround me in protective fifth dimensional light

Visualise Archangel Michael placing light and wisdom in your throat chakra so that you will know how to respond to any negative talk. See yourself surrounded in a bubble of high frequency energy that doesn't permit fear and low frequency thought forms to slip in.

What positives would you wish for this person? If you are not wishing them anything positive stay with yourself first!

<u>Proxy tapping for someone else who has an addiction</u>

So often people who have addictions have other people in their lives that would love to help. Sometimes the need to help can become unhealthy as in the case of co-dependency where there is an 'I need you to need me,' thing going on. But if you know someone with an addiction and would love to help why not tap for them? Beware: don't get tangled up in other people's addictions, at the end of the day they are a free agent and change comes from them and only them. Trying to help needs to be balanced with a wise degree of detachment.

HC: Archangel Raphael please help .... with their addictive behaviours
HC: I really worry about them and wish them well

HC: Please help them to seek the help they need

TH: Thank you Archangel Michael for cutting any cords which I may have formed through my concern for this person

TE: Or any cords which they have formed with me

EB: I know cords are not helpful for them or for me

SE: I can send my best wishes without getting into any toxic exchange

UE: I know it's their decision

UN: And it's really hard for me to watch sometimes

CH: I really wish that I could help

CB: And I don't want to make things worse

Th: I can get so fearful when I think about them

If: I'd really like to stay positive and visualise them doing well

Mf: Handing that choice back over to them

Rf: It's down to them and not me

Bf: Releasing any arguments about that now

KC: thank you Archangel Raphael for surrounding this person in love and healing

HC: I detach now and allow you to continue this work as needed, thank you

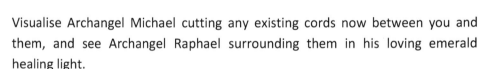

Visualise Archangel Michael cutting any existing cords now between you and them, and see Archangel Raphael surrounding them in his loving emerald healing light.

 If you are comfortable with this technique, you may write to that person's guardian angel and channel a response, asking for the guidance of the angels in doing so. Channelling angel messages is where you ask the angels to let their messages flow through you, and in this case you write down what comes through, without over-thinking it. Most people like to burn the letters afterwards. Always ask that your channelling be for the highest good of all concerned. Messages from angels are always loving and uplifting.

Chapter Summary:

● Our unhealthy patterns and addictions have been serving us at a lower ego level, which is why they can be hard to change. There is something in it for us.

● These patterns can be the cause and/or the result of difficult emotions.

● If you are resistive about dealing with an addiction or unhealthy pattern tap for this first, *think about moving up the SUE Scale one point at a time.*

● It's normal to feel resistant about changing or dealing with it.

● If you are dealing with an addiction sometimes it's best to get help rather than facing it alone.

● Archangel Raphael helps eliminate addictions.

● Archangel Zadkiel works with the Violet Flame which is great for removing fear-based energy that can be associated with addictions and unhealthy patterns.

● Archangel Gabriel works to purify our energy and gives us new insights.

● Practising the healing work for 30 days to make long-standing changes and beyond it if this feels right. Also at sporadic intervals as needed.

● Positive tapping for future aspects doing the new behaviour is a very useful way to end a session where a problem has complexity. It resolves the 'wild goose chase' effect where looking at problem goes off on many tangents in a session... common with addictions and unwanted behaviour patterns.

● If it is someone else's problem behaviour, you can proxy tap for them or tap for how it affects you, or both. Archangel Michael helps us to cut cords of fear attaching us to other people and their addictions.

Chapter 7: Healing Ancestral Patterns & Past Life Experiences

Bert Hellinger taught the therapy world that our childhood is not the end point of our psychological influence as regards the family. Tragedies and difficulties in the family that occurred a long time ago can wreak their energetic havoc on generations to come. The difficulties of the parents being mirrored by the children, and the grandchildren and so on. The child is loyal to the family and so takes on the problems as an unconscious way of being faithful and of belonging. Fields of energy have memory and influence and until that energy is cleared the patterns may still pass down along the generations repeating themselves. Originally it was believed that this only happened because of nurture theories; monkey see - monkey do. But Hellinger pointed out that it was the energy that passed on, and the recipient newer generation often had no idea of the ancestral connection, and it may originate from way back.

"When the family has been brought into its natural order, the individual can leave it behind him while still feeling the strength of his family supporting him. Only when the connection to his family is acknowledged, and the person's responsibility seen clearly and then distributed, can the individual feel unburdened and go about his personal affairs without anything from the past weighing him down or holding him back."

- Bert Hellinger

Family constellation work is where a group (who usually doesn't even know the family in question) are asked in a workshop environment to represent the family members. Themes are played out, resulting in depression, anxiety, illness, aloneness, alcoholism, anger etc, being on occasions miraculously healed. I was in such a workshop, representing someone's uncle and suddenly became aware of discomfort in my leg and was told afterwards that the uncle had trouble with this leg. And another whereby all the representatives were in floods of tears over the death of the father whom they had never met. It is very powerful. I have also seen this work being done without a large group whereby the family members are represented by shells, stones and suchlike. With the angels and Energy EFT to hand we can achieve powerful healing for ancestral patterns too.

Addressing the Angels in your Ancestral Healing Energy EFT work

If you want to represent people in the family you can use stones, shells or any-thing suitable to place on a surface where you can recognise who is who. I sug-gest working in an Energy EFT team, with an experienced practitioner. Each of your ancestors has their own guardian angel, and there are more angels over-seeing the family and even more when you ask them to come on board. You can work with Archangels of your choice also. If you are worried about permission, or if certain family members just wouldn't be into this, ask the angels to oversee the whole process.

Here is a technique I have used in an Angel EFT workshop with great results.

Tap on the Ancestors Angel EFT Technique

Light a candle, clear the space, and invoke the angels. Dedicate the candle to your ancestors, living and in the spirit world.

Imagine your ancestors lined up behind you that might have experienced problems or unhelpful beliefs for whatever reason. As you tap on yourself imagine that your tapping is so powerful that it is tapping all the points also on these ancestors and helping them to release, back in time, and experience relief and clarity. Ask the angels to tap on the ancestors, living and dead, way back across generations on people you have never met and might not know their names. Other members of the Energy EFT team tap along also.

HC: I invoke my own guardian angels and all the angels working with me today to do this work. I call forward all the angels of my ancestors, living and dead to assist now.

I ask the angels to support me with this powerful clearing work as I release unhelpful beliefs and behaviours from my DNA and cellular memory.

I invite the light-selves of my ancestors, with the help of the angelic realm to tap with me to release that which no longer serves.

TH: Angels I welcome your assistance to clear these patterns of ……. deeply and completely now.

TE: I allow the free flow of love to myself and all of my family, in all directions of time, to release the energy of fear now and transmute it into love.

EB: Any behaviours that I may have inherited through my DNA, through behaviour modelling, or through karmic reckoning from my ancestral lineage are lovingly released.

SE: I now lovingly release the behaviours or beliefs that have been holding me back from my being and from my cellular memory.

UE: I call upon the angels to assist me in clearing these patterns and also offering relief to the ancestors who are willing, as we tap together as a means of releasing that which no longer serves.

UN: I know that by tapping on this fear together I am helping clear the pain of the past as well as anything that causes me pain or fear at this time.

CH: I call in even more light, allowing love to flow freely in its own intelligence.

CB: I open my heart to forgiveness towards myself.

Th: And anyone else in my ancestral lineage whom I'd like to forgive.

If: I open myself up to love and joy.

Mf: And all of the blessings which will naturally follow from releasing this fear.

Rf: I invite angelic light into my auric field and into that of my family.

Bf: And I express gratitude for the learning opportunities this family has given me.

KC: I expand my heart to take in even more love.

HC: I allow this healing to take its own logical form, and the learning and love to flow through my being.

Now Say: I allow blissful freedom, love, blessings and peace for myself and my ancestral line in all directions of time.

I now lovingly detach and trust in the process of any ongoing work with my ancestors, and the angels working with them.

You can place your hands crossed over your chest as a gesture of detachment, as well as any team members.

Spend a little time afterwards in meditation, be aware of any guidance the angels have for you and keep a notepad to hand to note anything down that is useful. Clear and ground yourself, and detach again.

Energy Blocks from Past Life Experiences

Some people have a feeling or a sense of knowing that past life experiences are somehow holding them back in this life. Brian Weiss, a psychiatrist who used hypnotherapy with his clients to uncover past life blocks, writes about this in his books, including *Many Lives, Many Masters*. Whether our past life memories or feelings are fact or simply metaphors for the unconscious mind, we can clear the energy blockages with Angel EFT.

Case Example: Viv had a psychic knowing that she was burned at the stake in a past life for being a witch, or so-called because her beliefs didn't fit in with current societal ones of the time. Women were not meant to be independent and wise like she was. Viv felt she had been a knowledgeable herbalist, and many of the villagers had come to her instead of the doctor as she had a great capacity to heal. She was tried by the law and found guilty of witchcraft. She was publicly burned at the stake, and she believes that in this current life she often holds herself back because of her fear carried through from the past life. 'I hide my light,' she complained, 'I don't want to be ostracised.'

Viv was a talented and intuitive card reader and people would go to her for readings, which she never charged for despite the help they evidently gave people. People would come away feeling much better, she was a natural healer and lifted people, helping them to see things more clearly. She wanted to make a job of it and earn an income but had all sorts of negative self-talk which crippled her from moving forward. She was living on very little, working part time as a home help, and could have set up a small business for herself legally and without too much difficulty. She dreamed of doing so, but felt terrified about it. We did some past life release work with Archangel Raziel and Archangel Raphael whom she felt very attuned to.

<u>An example of how to go about clearing past life stuff:</u>

Light a candle, clear a space

Tap on, or simply say this out loud with hands on your heart healing position (HC)

Archangels Raphael, Michael and Raziel please assist me now

I wish to clear anything from my past life or lives that is blocking me from going forward

I choose to allow love to flow freely and let go of unhealthy beliefs

I send love and healing to my past aspects in all of this lifetime and any other ones where I have aspects that are hurting

Please facilitate this healing now, angels

Help me to move forward

Cutting any cords of fear now that my aspects have been experiencing

Sending love to myself and releasing those involved with love

Whomever may have hurt my past aspects was doing the best they could at that time according to their level of consciousness

I release all the resentment from my being that I possibly can at this time and allow more love to flow through me

Thank you Angels

Finish with some time with eyes closed connecting in to the angels, and be aware of energy changes and any messages or info that comes through. Write things down afterwards.

Chapter Summary:

● Energetic links are formed across generations, we can use energy work to release old patterns that have been energetically passed on.

● You can use stones, shells or other items to represent ancestors in your ancestral Angel EFT work, and it may be helpful to work in an Energy EFT team.

● *Tap on the Ancestors* Angel EFT technique is a powerful exercise to help release problems at an ancestral level.

● We may also carry energies from past lives, and if we have memories of past lives, or even think we do, we can work with these in Angel EFT with our intention to clear it.

Chapter 8: The Chakras and Angel EFT

We have many chakras in and around our physical body; these are energy centres where energy pathways cross over many times. Some are large and some are small. Small ones are in the feet for example. In this chapter I look briefly at the seven third dimensional chakras. I just give a general outline and there is much more to be said about them. A good knowledge of how to balance the chakras is a really good asset in terms of having balanced healthy energy and enjoying life. People have used yoga, crystals, food types, other energy healing modalities and even certain coloured clothes to help balance the chakras. Here we take a little look at the chakras and how to balance them with Angel EFT. As always in this book, one size does not fit all, and you should tailor your Energy EFT rounds for the issue you are working on.

<u>The Seven Major Chakras</u>

Traditionally seven major chakras were taught about, these are the crown chakra, third eye or brow chakra, the throat chakra, the heart chakra, the solar plexus chakra, the sacral chakra and the base chakra. These are positioned like so in the diagram and radiate out to the front and the rear of the body with the crown at the top radiating up and the base radiating down towards the earth. Chakras can get clogged up and either shrunken or over-expanded, they can get tears in them, they can close up. When we look after our chakras it has a beneficial effect on our life. Each of the seven represents an aspect of our health and if out of sync will manifest in certain ways of ill-functioning.

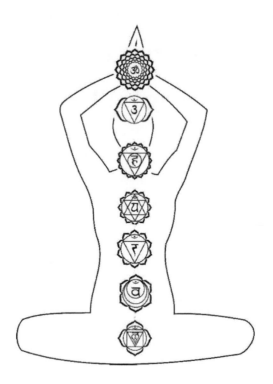

Crown Chakra

The crown chakra is our spiritual centre and link to the heavens. In good health we feel connected, a sense of flow and knowing why we are here. If somebody has cut off their spirituality so will it appear as a closed crown chakra and they will experience unbalance. It could manifest in many ways, including headaches, migraine, feeling bored or not on the right path, being overly-materialistic and identifying with possessions. When we over-intellectualise imbalance also occurs in the crown chakra. The physical aspects of the crown chakra include the pineal gland.

Angel EFT to open and balance the crown chakra

Three deep breaths at heart centre

HC: Archangel Jophiel assist me now in opening and balancing my crown chakra

TH: Opening and balancing my crown chakra

TE: I am open to divine light and wisdom

EB: I am a beloved child of God and am able to receive this light

SE: I am open to learning more about how to assist my crown chakra in its perfect balance

UE: Releasing any blocks now

UN: Nourishing my connection with spirit and my higher self

CH: Thank you Archangel Jophiel for helping me to do this work

CB: My crown chakra serves my entire energy system

Th: As an opening to all the other chakras from the Divine Source

If: When it is open and balanced I can experience bliss

Mf: Bliss that is here for me

Rf: Healthy spiritual balance that's just right for me

Bf: Thank you Archangel Jophiel

KC: I am open to your guidance and wisdom

HC: Thank you for my perfectly balanced and healthy crown chakra

What else would you wish for your healthy vibrant crown chakra? Tap on the positives, finishing at HC with 'thank you Archangel Jophiel.'

Visualisation for the crown chakra generally

Tune into the crown chakra now, the crown of the head radiating up. Sense what the energy there is like right now. Have an awareness, without judgement. Ask Archangel Jophiel to place a violet and white ball of light into the crown centre now, see the energies meld together and take some deep breaths. Allow the new energy to settle, and make a note of any messages or intuition that occurs. See the ball of light settling in and expanding up and out. You are fully connected to your higher self and the Divine, the Universe supports you. Allow this light from the crown chakra to really anchor now, connecting up to a stream of white light from above. Welcome the light into the body and out into the aura. Take some comfortable breaths here. Now visualise the petals of the crown chakra opening fully, blossoming and radiating up.

Tune in and note down anything you want to remember. Ground your energy and ask your angel to pull your aura and your chakras in close to the body to a level that is comfortable and appropriate for you.

Third Eye (or brow) Chakra

The third eye chakra is open when we are born and are young children but shrinks down in many cases in societies that do not nurture trusting your own intuition and developing psychic ability. Being psychic is our birth right. We may not be card readers or fortune tellers but we are all capable of seeing or sensing our guides and angels, and receiving psychic information if we so wish. This has been suppressed in many societies, and children of school age stopped seeing and sensing things as they were taught to doubt or dismiss the things they see. Psychics have been feared and persecuted in the past, and there still exists a stigma or fear energy around even the word psychic for some people.

Even very spiritual people sometimes have mixed feelings about becoming more psychic, they want to but they are afraid and so block themselves with the fear they hold. You can work with the angels to release this block, even to explore where the fear originates from and decide whether it is warranted or relevant any more.

The physical aspect of the third eye chakra are the eyes, the base of the skull, the nose and sinuses, the face and the cerebellum and central nervous system.

Angel EFT to open and balance the third eye chakra

Three deep breaths at heart centre
HC: Archangel Raphael assist me now in opening and balancing my third eye chakra
TH: Opening and balancing my third eye chakra

TE: I am open to divine insights and being able to manifest that which is for my highest good

EB: It is safe for me to access my intuition and connect with my loving, high frequency guides and angels

SE: I ask that I see into the higher realms and not into lower frequencies which do not concern me or benefit me

UE: Releasing any veils or blocks now

UN: Anything from this life or any other

CH: Thank you Archangel Raphael for helping me to do this work

CB: My third eye chakra assists me in living a healthy and balanced life

Th: When it is open and balanced, I can manifest the things I dream of

If: I can access my divine wisdom and intuition

Mf: Which is there for me whenever I want it

Rf: I invite loving high frequency intuitions now which I will easily pick up on

Bf: Thank you Archangel Raphael

KC: I am open to your guidance and wisdom

HC: Thank you for my perfectly balanced and healthy third eye chakra

Visualisation for the third eye chakra generally

Tune into the third eye chakra now, the centre of the forehead radiating out to the front and also out behind your head. Sense what the energy there is like right now. Make a mental note of it, without judgement. Ask Archangel Raphael to place an indigo ball of light into the brow chakra now, see the energies meld together and take some deep breaths. Allow the new energy to settle, and make a note of any messages or intuition that occurs. See the ball of light settling in and expanding. You are fully connected to your higher self and are opening up to your intuition. Allow this light from the third eye chakra to really blossom now, strengthening your ability to manifest and be intuitive beyond ego. Send light to your hopes and dreams. Take some comfortable breaths here as you visualise the things you really want, with the support of Archangel Raphael. Tune in and make a note of anything you want to remember. Ground your energy and ask your angel to pull your aura and your chakras in close to the body to a level that is comfortable and appropriate for you.

You could carry on at this point, tapping in some more positives for your third eye chakra if you feel it would be of benefit.

<u>Throat Chakra</u>

The throat chakra is our communication centre. We are able to speak our truth with love, and express our creativity freely when this chakra is in balance. Archangel Michael is responsible for this chakra. Coughs, sore throats, and other ill health in this area may indicate a throat chakra imbalance. Often when people feel they can't express how they feel this chakra suffers. When it is open and balanced we communicate easily, and our creative projects flourish.

The throat, the vocal cords, neck, bronchial tubes, trachea, oesophagus, jaw, arms, nose and teeth are connected physically to the throat chakra.

Angel EFT to open and balance the throat chakra

Three deep breaths at heart centre
HC: Archangel Michael assist me now in opening and balancing my throat chakra
TH: Opening and balancing my throat chakra
TE: I step into my power to lovingly speak my truth
EB: Everybody benefits when I speak my truth with love
SE: Releasing any old doubts or fears around that now
UE: Any beliefs that I should just 'put up and shut up.'
UN: That never benefited me or anyone else
CH: I release with Archangel Michaels help anything from this life or any other that has hindered the development of my throat chakra now
CB: Thank you Archangel Michael for your healing blue light which surrounds my throat chakra now
Th: All communication systems that I am responsible for are now cleared in a safe and loving way
If: I flourish in my divine creativity

Mf: The creativity that is my birth right
Rf: I communicate clearly and easily
Bf: Led by the beloved Archangel Michael
KC: I am open to your guidance and wisdom
HC: Thank you Archangel Michael for my perfectly balanced and healthy throat chakra

What positives would your throat chakra benefit from now?

Visualisation for the throat chakra generally
Tune into the throat chakra now at the base of the neck. Sense what the energy there is like right now. Make a mental note of it, without judgement. Ask Archangel Michael to place a deep blue ball of light into the throat centre now, see the energies meld together and take some deep breaths. Allow the new energy to settle, and make a note of any messages or intuition that occurs. See the ball of light settling in and expanding out. You are fully supported by your angels to speak your truth and communicate effectively, and your creativity flows freely. Allow this light from the throat chakra to expand out even more, connecting up to a stream of white light from above. Welcome the light into the body and out into the aura. Take some comfortable breaths here. Now visualise the petals of the crown chakra opening fully, blossoming and radiating up.

Tune in and make a note of anything you want to remember. Ground your energy and ask your angel to pull your aura and your chakras in close to the body to a level that is comfortable and appropriate for you.
Case Example: Michelle was working with me on the anger she was experiencing. We spent some time de-stressing in the beginning, because when I asked her what had been going on there had been so many things and talking about them got her into a stressed state. As she was telling me about some of them she began coughing. 'This always happens; my throat constricts it's as though there are angry words stuck in the throat.' We did a visualisation at this point.

123

Close your eyes and be aware of your body being supported by the chair. Imagine that there is a golden stream of angelic light, flowing in through the crown chakra and into the energy meridians and energy body. Invite this light into the physical body; let it light up every cell in the body. Relax as this light fills you up and offers you a sense of peace. Invite Archangel Michael to help now with your throat chakra specifically, whilst other angels work in the background on the other chakras as needed. Archangel Michael is healing your throat chakra and you silently use the affirmation 'I speak my truth with love.'

We then completed some tapping, similar to the round outlined above with Archangel Michael and the throat, and then completed a further visualisation:

Still with eyes closed imagine your energy body as a shining light, see yourself looking confident and assured. Breathe in the energy for a few more moments and allow it to settle. Gently open your eyes and check in.

Michelle was much calmer and able to see her own role in responding to the drama of those around her, and her own responsibility to be assertive and have good boundaries.

Heart Chakra

The heart chakra is associated with the colour green, and sometimes with a pink centre. It is the love centre. When the heart chakra is in radiant health we love ourselves and others easily. We see the best in ourselves and others. Out of balance, we can withhold love from ourselves, and typically this means we cannot love others. Here we find ourselves closed off, untrusting, judgemental of self and others. Forgiveness heals the heart chakra.

Grief is another emotion which manifests in the heart. People feeling broken hearted have heart chakra problems. This doesn't mean however that because you are grieving - and there is no quick-fix - that you can't help heal your heart chakra. Often in bereavements of someone close, a part of us doesn't want to feel too much better for fear that that would be disloyal to the loved one that died. So we hold on to the sadness, sometimes wearing it in our aura like a dark veil. We can still help the heart with Angel EFT even if we don't want to let go or move on.

For this sample round I have focused just on grieving but you can use Energy EFT for the heart chakra for many heart issues; the break-up of a relationship, self-worth and self-criticism, to attract a partner or more romance into your current relationship, and more.

Physically the heart chakra is connected to the heart, upper back, thorax, breasts, lungs, blood and circulation, skin, immune system, hands and arms. Archangel Chamuel is the heart chakra Archangel.

Angel EFT to help open and balance the heart chakra in bereavement

Three deep breaths at heart centre

HC: Archangel Chamuel assist me now in opening and balancing my heart chakra

TH: I accept love and light into my heart chakra now

TE: I feel so sad about .... (person who has died)

EB: I feel so heartbroken

SE: A part of me feels that I should be suffering this way and so I block myself from feeling any better

UE: It's as though my heart ought to be broken otherwise it might mean that I don't care

UN: But maybe I can allow myself to grieve in a less painful way and still feel loyal and loving towards ....

CH: Archangel Chamuel thank you for guiding me towards the right help and assistance in healing my heart as best I can under the circumstances

CB: It is right that I should experience some relief

Th: I am open to learning how to gradually, and in my own time, heal my heart chakra

If: I wish the very best for ....

Mf: I do not wish them to have trouble crossing over because they feel tethered by my sadness

Rf: I send them so much love and best wishes

Bf: Assisted by the beloved Archangel Chamuel

KC: I am open to high frequency guidance and wisdom

HC: Thank you Archangel Chamuel for your loving work on my heart chakra

What might be some positives for the heart chakra you could tap on for grieving now? Keep going.

 I mentioned in this round about spirits having trouble crossing over because of being held back by a loved one's sadness. You can use or omit this, whatever feels right according to your beliefs.

Grief is very painful, and for some there is possibly no cure or shortcuts to feeling less sad, other than the passage of time. Energy EFT can help release blocks to the flow of energy which may in turn relive some of the grief symptoms or reduce their intensity.

Visualisation for the heart chakra generally
Tune into the heart space now, the centre of the chest. Sense what the energy there is like right now. Make a mental note of it, without judgement. Ask Archangel Chamuel to place a green ball of light with a pink centre into the heart centre now, see the energies meld together and take some deep breaths. Allow the new energy to settle, and make a note of any messages or intuition that occurs. See the ball of light settling in and expanding out in all directions. Your heart is filled with love. Allow this love from the heart chakra to expand out into every part of your body, and then beyond it into the aura. Take some comfortable breaths here. Now imagine sending out love to somebody, or an animal or place that needs it. You have the ability, with your intention, to send the energy of love at no cost to your own energy, when you ask the angels to support you. There is plenty to go around.

Tune in and make a note of anything you want to remember. Ground your energy and ask your angel to pull your aura and your chakras in close to the body to a level that is comfortable and appropriate for you.

Solar Plexus Chakra

The Solar Plexus chakra is at third dimension associated with a sunny yellow and is governed by Archangel Uriel. This is our power centre. If the power centre is out of balance we may feel weak and sluggish, and unassertive, being treated like a doormat. It can also be out of balance at the other extreme, people who are overpowering and dictatorial, misusing their power to exploit others.

The physical aspects are the liver, the gallbladder, spleen, kidneys and the stomach and the digestive system.

Angel EFT to open and balance the solar plexus chakra, particularly if the energy is weak and the person is not feeling powerful:

Three deep breaths at heart centre

HC: Archangel Uriel assist me now in opening and balancing my solar plexus chakra

TH: I invite the light of the sun to fill up my solar plexus now

TE: I step into my power in a healthy and balanced way

EB: Everybody benefits when I stand in my power as I choose to use it wisely and with love

SE: Releasing any old doubts or fears around that now

UE: Any beliefs that I should give my power away to other people

UN: That never benefited me or them, in fact it sometimes enabled their bad behaviour

CH: I release with Archangel Uriel's help anything from this life or any other that has hindered the development of my solar plexus chakra now

CB: Thank you Archangel Uriel for your love and guidance in helping me to step into my power with love

Th: I am open to learning new ways of being around standing in my power

If: I welcome gentle opportunities now so that I can practise it

Mf: I accept golden yellow light into my solar plexus, I see as it expands, radiating out like the sun

Rf: Thank you Archangel Uriel for your loving guidance and assistance

Bf: I am open to signs and guidance now

KC: Beautiful shining solar plexus chakra

HC: Thank you Archangel Uriel for my perfectly balanced and healthy solar plexus chakra

Visualisation for the solar plexus chakra generally

Tune into the solar plexus now, the centre of the base of the rib cage. Sense what the energy there is like right now. Make a mental note of it, without judgement. Ask Archangel Uriel to place a ball of golden yellow light into the solar plexus now, see the energies meld together and take some deep breaths. Allow the new energy to settle, and make a note of any messages or intuition that occurs. See the ball of light settling in and expanding out in all directions. Your solar plexus is filled with bright radiant energy. Allow this sunny energy to expand out into every part of your body, and then beyond it into the aura. Take some comfortable breaths.

Tune in and make a note of anything you want to remember. Ground your energy and ask your angel to pull your aura and your chakras in close to the body to a level that is comfortable and appropriate for you.

Sacral Chakra

The Sacral Chakra is located in the lower abdomen, associated with the colour orange and Archangel Gabriel works with his chakra. Some of the issues connected are: pleasure, sweetness, sexuality and intimacy, creativity, going with the flow and enjoying life and the things you have achieved. The physical body corresponding connections are the hips, lower back, the gonads, bladder, kidneys, stomach, large intestine, pelvis, appendix and the body fluids. We tend to hold addictions in the sacral chakra if it is out of balance.
Angel EFT to open and balance the sacral chakra

Three deep breaths at heart centre
HC: Archangel Gabriel assist me now in opening and balancing my sacral chakra
TH: I invite pure divine light to fill up my sacral chakra now

TE: I balance these energies now with the help of my angels and Archangel Gabriel

EB: Releasing anything that may have been blocking me from this

SE: I allow pure health to enhance my creative flow

UE: I allow well-being and joy in my sexuality

UN: Pure divine light shining on my relationships and sociability

CH: Being open to any intuition or guidance from my angels

CB: Thank you Archangel Gabriel for your loving, healing energy

Th: I allow myself to experience pleasure in my life

If: I invite sweetness into my being

Mf: I celebrate my achievements and who I Am

Rf: Thank you Archangel Gabriel for your loving guidance and assistance

Bf: I am open to any guidance now for the ongoing health of my sacral chakra

KC: Beautiful shining healthy energy centre

HC: Thank you Archangel Gabriel for my perfectly balanced and healthy sacral chakra

Visualisation for the sacral chakra generally

Tune into the sacral chakra, about two inches below the navel. Sense what the energy there is like right now. Make a mental note of it, without judgement. Ask Archangel Gabriel to place an orange ball of light into the sacral chakra now, see the energies meld together and take some deep breaths. Allow the new energy to settle, and make a note of any messages or intuition that occurs. See the ball of light settling in and expanding out in all directions. Your sacral chakra is filled with love and tenderness. Allow this to expand out into every part of your body, and then beyond it into the aura. Take some comfortable breaths here. Now tune in to any blocks that you may have experienced around this centre which may have come to your awareness in the tapping round. If you didn't have any blocks remain for a few moments in the expansion. Place any symbols you think may be useful here. For example, if you have been emotionally needy maybe the symbol of angel wings to help you feel reassured, or for sexuality a fertility symbol or an angel or love or romance.

Tune in and make a note of anything you want to remember. Ground your energy and ask your angel to pull your aura and your chakras in close to the body to a level that is comfortable and appropriate for you.

Base Chakra

The base chakra at this dimension is associated with a beautiful ruby red in its healthy state. Archangel Gabriel also looks after this chakra, which radiates downward from the base of the spine and perineum. Our base chakra is connected with our basic survival needs for shelter, warmth, food and money. If we are having any problems with our home or living space, it can affect the base chakra. If our home is messy or something needs fixing it can manifest imbalance there. Also if we are ungrounded the base chakra is out of balance. Spiritual energy is dominant in the upper chakras, but if we neglect to strengthen our base chakra symptoms such as being spaced out with our head in the clouds can mean we need to work on the base.

The physical connections are the legs, feet, spine, bones, teeth, nails, anus, rectum, colon, prostate, blood and cellular structuring and the most primitive, reptilian part of the brain.

Angel EFT to open and balance the base chakra

Three deep breaths at heart centre
HC: Archangel Gabriel assist me now in opening and balancing my base chakra
TH: I invite sparkling ruby red light to flow into my base chakra now
TE: I assist myself in being grounded and centred
EB: I invite balance into my life
SE: Allowing myself to feel safe and to belong
UE: I easily attract enough money into my life
UN: My material needs are blissfully met
CH: I release with Archangel Gabriel's help anything that has hindered the full functioning of my base chakra now
CB: Thank you Archangel Gabriel for your love and support
Th: I am open to learning new ways of being strong in my base chakra

If: I support myself in being grounded

Mf: My energy is strong and I easily complete the tasks I need to do today

Rf: Thank you Archangel Gabriel for your loving guidance and assistance

Bf: I am open to abundance and having a wonderful home space

KC: Beautiful radiant base chakra

HC: Thank you Archangel Gabriel for my perfectly balanced and healthy base chakra

Visualisation for the base chakra generally

Tune into the base chakra, radiating down towards the earth from the base of the spine. Sense what the energy there is like right now. Make a mental note of it, without judgement. Ask Archangel Gabriel to place a ball of shimmering ruby red light into the base chakra now, see the energies meld together and take some deep breaths. Allow the new energy to settle, and make a note of any messages or intuition that occurs. See the ball of light settling in and expanding out and down. Your base chakra is filled with bright radiant energy. Allow this ruby red energy to flow and radiate down towards the earth, making you feel very centred, safe and grounded. Take some comfortable breaths here.

Tune in and make a note of anything you want to remember. Keep tapping for positives for the base chakra, finishing with 'thank you Archangel Gabriel on the heart centre. Some positives for base chakra might be: mountain energy; earth energy; strength; roots; tree energy; homeliness and suchlike. Whatever *you* need. Ground your energy and ask your angel to pull your aura and your chakras in close to the body to a level that is comfortable and appropriate for you.

Chapter Summary:

● We have many chakras in and around our physical body; major and minor chakras, these are energy centres where energy pathways cross over many times.

● When we look after our 7 major chakras it has a beneficial effect on our life. Each of the seven represents an aspect of our health and if out of sync will manifest in certain ways of ill-functioning.

● Each major chakra is connected to parts of the physical body.

● The crown chakra radiates up and is responsible for our connection to spirit.

● The third eye chakra is connected with our intuition and ability to manifest.

● The throat chakra is our communication centre.

● The heart chakra is the love centre.

● The solar plexus chakra governs our sense of power.

● The sacral chakra is connected with our sexuality and self-esteem.

● The base chakra represents our basic survival needs, home and finances.

● Different Archangels are helpers of different chakras.

Chapter 9: Healthy Joyous Body

In Energy EFT we don't ever promise people a cure for their illnesses and ailments. To do so would be unethical, and besides we can never predict how a person will respond since we are all unique. That being said, there is an undeniable link between having healthy energy flow and a healthy body and mind. So if we can work on the energy system, it is likely to have an effect on the physical also. With Angel EFT we may also call upon the angels through visualisation and other connecting exercises to help us with our insights as to what is happening with the body, and what it needs. For a person who is experiencing physical illness, whether cancer or tendonitis, we can ask the angels for more understanding.

Christian Flèche, the leading researcher and practitioner in the field of biogenealogy, explains that the "activation of illness" is the body's reaction to unresolved events that are frozen in time. These unresolved traumas affect the body on the cellular level and manifest in minor as well as more serious chronic conditions. In *The Biogenealogy Sourcebook*, Flèche systematically chronicles all the major organs of the body and specifies the types of emotional conflicts that lead to illness in those areas. In Angel EFT this affords us many opportunities to discover what might have caused the activation, by asking our angels to shed more light for us if this is for our highest good. Then we can tap, along with the angels, to release the trauma from the past aspect, and all the associated energy that has manifested in the physical body is likely to benefit.

Whilst scientifically difficult to prove, the idea is well documented. For example, Louise Hay illustrates in her book *Heal Your Body* how a sore throat may mean inability to express yourself or angry words stuck in the throat, along with other authors. Either way having awareness empowers us to make room for change or different decision making. It is possible that it's not so straight forward as one symptom being always attributed to the same thing going on in every person's energy, since we are complex beings. In my experience, keeping an open mind and asking the angels for more wisdom about where the ill-health experience comes from opens the door to newfound insight and healing.

General Angel EFT round for more insights in getting well:

Three deep breaths at heart centre
HC: Angels I would like to know more about how to help myself to get better as far as possible please
TH: Archangel Raphael assist me now
TE: Healing Angels I call upon your loving support
EB: Surround me with your healing light
SE: I am open to learning more about how to help myself
UE: How to act kindly towards my body
UN: To become aware of and to heal any unhealthy patterns which may have contributed to my current experience of pain
CH: To clear any energetic blocks to my experiencing radiant health
CB: Help me to release any toxic emotions or energies now
Th: Help me to become aware of any dietary changes which would benefit my body
If: And the willpower to integrate these
Mf: My being sick is not serving anyone
Rf: I allow myself to open up to healing now
Bf: Thank you Archangel Raphael
KC: Thank you Healing Angels
HC: Angels of Healing I thank you for these new insights and wisdom

Spend some time now with eyes closed; you may leave your hand at the heart centre if this is comfortable. Connecting in with the angels and become aware of any ideas, any insights that may come to mind. If any images of what's going on in the body or energy body arise, keep tapping, keep asking for healing and insight.

Affirmations

Tapping on the positive: *Thank you angels for my healthy happy body* is another way to invite in more positive energy around your health. Affirmations can help us to notice what doesn't feel true to us, and then we can tap on that. I have those two ways of using affirmations: for retraining the mind to think positively about something I am manifesting, and also to highlight my resistance and work through it.

For example, if you are using the affirmation 'I have a healthy body and am full of vitality,' and repeating this helps you to feel this way then well and good. But if thoughts pop up when you say it such as *'no I don't, I'll never feel that way,'* the door is open for you to explore that belief and help heal any resistance the mind is presenting.

Test out the following affirmations and see how they are for you right now:

I am beautiful
I am healthy
I am graceful
I am confident in how I look
I am so grateful for my body

If you want to feel more of these, think again of the SUE Scale. Ask the question: how do I move up just one place? Often just asking that question promotes a move upward, since it promotes solution focused thought. Then we are able to aim Angel EFT at it to progress even further.

Food and Fuelling the Happy Body

We use food to fuel the body, but we also use it for pleasure and gratification. In most of western society we use too much food for our bodies. This isn't helped by food manufacturers creating unhealthy, yet addictive foods, and marketing them and making those the ones that are always on offer or shining brightly at the supermarket. For those who really enjoy food, it takes a lot of discipline to eat a healthy diet. I speak for myself here, but most of us know when we have eaten something that really hasn't done any good for our body. Perhaps we ate it out of comfort or 'being sociable' like at celebrations when everyone else is having it. Of course tapping and bringing in the angels opens up opportunities for change and assistance with this.

The way we prepare and eat food matters also. Eating on the go, mindlessly, in front of the TV, whilst driving or suchlike are ways of being disconnected to the feeding of our*selves*. Most times if were feeding a baby we would interact with the baby, not completely ignore them while we shovel in the spoonfuls. We should also afford this same behaviour for ourselves, in that being present while we eat is a way of nurturing the self and improving our relationship with food and nourishment. Preparing a meal with love. Presenting a meal, even if only for ourselves, with care and attention.

Sai Maa Lakshmi Devi, a world-renowned spiritual master, healer and humanitarian speaks of the energy and intention we use while preparing food and the power of blessing the food. Similarly, in my reiki and angel trainings, I learned this. Taking the time just before you eat, just to place your hands above the plate mentally blessing the food you are about to eat raises its frequency, and thus yours. You can use the 'angels blessing your healing hands with golden light' technique when you are cooking or blessing your food. Imagine you are stirring love into your soups and ask the angels to bless your dishes. There are lots of ways you can do it, intention is key.

Dr Masaru Emoto famously demonstrated the effect of specific thoughts directed at water, and using high speed photography, the crystals that formed showed brilliant complex and colourful snowflake patterns when exposed to loving words. Water exposed to negative words formed incomplete asymmetrical patterns with dull colours. If we are made up of at least 55% water, then perhaps we should take extra care to use loving thoughts and words about ourselves rather than negative ones. I have found when I affixed images and corresponding words of the beautiful water crystals with the intention of blessing the water to water bottles, my children and I noticed a different taste and energy in the water.

For overeating I have included a round in Chapter 6 with Archangels Raphael and Gabriel. For bringing more light into the food you eat you could start the day with a round asking the angels of your choice to guide you to higher light bearing foods, to help you to bless your foods. Also for releasing unhealthy cravings, and for motivation in sticking to a healthy diet.

Not Accepting the Body

Some of us have become quite disconnected with the body, by living in our heads all the time. There are a few reasons why this can be the case. Sometimes it's not being grounded. Sometimes when people dislike their body, as happens at times when the person was abused but also in many other situations, they disconnect from it, almost dismissing it is a part of them. They hate looking in the mirror, or picking out clothes. They may overeat or treat their body without kindness in other ways. It could also have roots in adolescence, particularly with girls, who find they do not look anything like the women on the TV or in the magazines, and so they reject their body. It must be wrong after all, since the media doesn't show any ones like it.

Angel EFT round for accepting the body with Archangel Uriel:

Three deep breaths at heart centre
HC: Archangel Uriel please help me to accept my body
TH: I ask for your shining light of confidence now
TE: To radiate through my physical body
EB: Help me to release any old unhelpful beliefs now
SE: So that I can accept the body I have
UE: Enjoy being in this body
UN: Help me to gently become aware of anything that has been blocking this so that I can work through it
CH: In a way that is safe and acceptable for me
CB: Help me to let go of unhelpful ways of speaking and thinking about my body
Th: I choose to make peace with my body
If: Thank you Archangel Uriel for bringing this peace to me

Mf: On an ongoing basis

Rf: Filling me up with peace and confidence

Bf: Accepting my body and feeling grateful to have one

KC: Thank you for this confidence

HC: Thank you for this healing

Now what do you need to move even higher up the SUE Scale for this issue? What does +10 look like or sound like? Keep tapping on positives, finishing with 'thank you Archangel Uriel', at HC.

For some people this can be a deep and long standing issue, and it may be best to work with a trained practitioner. Take note of the different things that come up and address them one at a time if needed.

Chapter Summary:

● Even though in Energy EFT we never make claims of cure, we know that if we work on the energy body the likelihood is that it will also benefit the physical body.

● Certain symptoms and illnesses may be linked to patterns, traumas or other things going on in our lives, as illustrated by Christian Flèche, Louise Hay and others.

● In Angel EFT we can ask the angels for more insight with the intention of improving our physical health. This could be about releasing unhealthy patterns, expressing our emotions, releasing trauma and being guided to healthier foods or other actions we can take.

● Affirmations work in two ways; in telling the subconscious mind to learn something new but also when there is a strong argument they demonstrate our resistance and give us a focus to work on with Angel EFT.

● Paying attention whilst eating, preparing food with love and blessing our food are all rituals which promote healthy energy around the food we eat and our relationship with nourishment.

● Sending loving thoughts and messages to water is believed to raise its frequency, and since we are made up of at least 55% water we could do the same for ourselves for the same reason.

● Non-acceptance of the body can be caused by a number of things but Angel EFT can help. For some people this is deep rooted and may be best tackled with an experienced practitioner, and one part at a time.

Chapter 10: Proxy Tapping – Healing Others, Aspects, Animals & Situations

The importance of proxy, or surrogate tapping should not be underestimated. It gives us the ability to help people and situations where teaching them to tap isn't an option. Notably, in Energy EFT proxy tapping is not described as sending healing. I sometimes refer to it as such here in Angel EFT, as many people who work with angels are healers and may like the idea that proxy tapping is like sending healing. And in many ways, it is, just not in the same way as Reiki or other healing modalities. Think of it rather as sending the gift of energy. You can do this via visualisation also, as well as tapping, for those who are good at visualising.

We can proxy tap for animals, our relationships, the workplace and for aspects of ourselves in the past and even in the future. With it, we can send healing to people or places faraway, and for things as vast as the planet itself. I love the way that I can help someone without having to explain the whole energy thing - for people that might just not be into it, or where there is a communication barrier. For me proxy tapping makes me feel as though I'm doing something in a situation where perhaps otherwise I am wondering how on earth I can help.

It is also a very effective way of sending healing to ourselves in the past when we were undergoing stresses or trauma. Can you imagine the changes in the world if when watching the news instead of worrying and getting into fear everyone did some proxy tapping to help the situation? We can make the choice to do this.

Ethical Considerations

In sending distance healing to a person there is a belief that you should get permission first, check if it's okay. That's good manners isn't it? However, I also believe that there are times when getting permission for whatever reason just isn't practical. And so I ask the angels that if the person does not want to receive the healing effect of the proxy tapping that it be used elsewhere, for something or someone that needs and accepts it. We don't always know what is for a person's highest good, but the angels do. Also when I do proxy tapping for someone else I check, using my intuition, if this is okay for me or not.

Sometimes when we have a strong desire to help someone else we need to check for cords of toxic energy exchange (see chapter 6 & 11). If there is a situation where we pick up a lot of toxic exchange for whatever reason, we can delegate to the angels by simply asking them to help the person or situation in question.

Detachment

The other consideration when we do proxy tapping for somebody else is that we have to let it go once we are done and trust. Otherwise, again, we might end up with toxic cords. It's okay to send healing a number of times but it's important to remember each time to detach. There are many techniques that help you to detach. Symbolically, you might cross your arms over your chest, with hands facing inwards to your shoulders and take a deep breath. You might say 'I now lovingly release this healing intention and detach myself, allowing it to flow,' or using words that are meaningful to you.

Healing Former Aspects of the Self

We can send healing to our former selves at moments in time when we really could have used some tapping, and perhaps hadn't even heard of it, or else weren't in a position to tap. The process of proxy tapping for the *aspect* is quite empowering and doesn't put the person back into 'being' that person in the trauma situation again. Thus sending them healing in a safe detached way. It is different to tapping for 'me at that time.' I can say 'sending healing for the aspect of Susan at that time,' and it doesn't get me right back into that painful, uncomfortable energy, as in the case of abreactions.

Tapping for a Former Aspect of Self with Archangel Jeremial

Light a candle for your former aspect if this feels right. It is a gesture of honouring the aspect and the angels.

Three deep breaths at heart centre

HC: Archangel Jeremial I call upon you to assist (use your name and the situation, e.g.: Margery at age thirteen being bullied by Sarah in the changing rooms)

TH: Helping this aspect to feel more empowered

TE: Sending her healing and love now

EB: Love and reassurance

SE: Sending her confidence and love

UE: Helping her to feel empowered

UN: Thank you Archangel Jeremial for allowing this healing to occur

CH: Sending her pure love and light

CB: Peace and calm now

Th: Allowing her to release fear from her energy now

If: Calm and understanding

Mf: Helping her to feel peaceful and protected no matter what

Rf: Peaceful and safe

Bf: Thank you Archangel Jeremial for your help

KC: Feelings of calm washing over her

Three deep breaths at heart centre

HC: Thank you for this powerful healing, I am free to detach now

Keep tapping on the positives, remembering to detach at the end.

143

Using Photographs in Aspect Work

Looking at old photographs of ourselves is a great guide to where we are at in terms of being accepting of ourselves, or being at peace with our past. We know that when there is an emotional *charge* when we look at old photos, that there is work we can do to help us heal. Thoughts such as 'look how slim I was then,' - not accepting the me that is now; or 'I was so stupid back then,' - not accepting the past aspect. We can use photographs in our healing work to clear away these bothersome non-accepting thoughts.

As a counsellor I have recommended to many clients to get a photograph of themselves as a child and place it in a lovely frame where they will see it regularly and can talk to that child –as you might in inner child work – and reassure that former self and express love. With Angel EFT we can take it to another level. Looking at old photos, even if they were taken just last year, will often stimulate a memory of what was happening in the energy body at that time. It may have been good, in which case frame it, put it somewhere you can see it and celebrate it. But if it wasn't so good thank it for the guidance. You can still frame it of course and use it in your tapping rounds to do healing for that aspect of you. Thank that photographer in your mind for taking a snapshot of that aspect so that you may help heal the energy of them.

Helping Animals

One day I was asked to watch a sheep that was supposedly in labour. I went down to see her in the field and she was very nervous of me. I am not the experienced farmer, and I really didn't want to make things worse, but I had been asked to keep an eye on her. She watched me with mistrust, her breathing was heavy. I got something to sit on and sat about six feet away from her using my own animal-reassuring voice to try to soothe her. I placed my hands on my heart centre and simply used the words Archangel Fhelyai.

I did a couple of rounds of this and then I left her there, watching her from a distance, not knowing what else to do, and not wanting to frighten her. The farmer returned later and intuitively rang the vet. It turned out that she had milk fever and was quite sick as opposed to being in labour. He gave her medicine. She began to recover against the odds. I will never know whether or not my tapping and asking Archangel Fhelyai helped, but it certainly helped me because I was able to do something when I otherwise would have felt inept. And she got better and soon afterwards gave birth to healthy twin lambs which was of course a real bonus.

About St Germain and the Violet Flame

I work with Ascended Masters as well as angels. Ascended Masters are spiritually enlightened beings who in past incarnations were ordinary human beings, but have undergone a series of initiations or spiritual transformations. Examples of Ascended Masters would be Jesus, Gautama Buddha, Lakshmi, Sanat Kumara, St Germain and many, many more. St Germain petitioned for the return of the Violet Flame for use by the whole of humanity in 1987 at the Harmonic Convergence, when many spiritual people prayed for help for our planet. The Violet Flame was granted, having been withdrawn since the devolution of Atlantis when it was being misused. You can use the Violet Flame for purifying yourself, your relationships, your life, your property, places. I use it to clear myself after healing work, and for other things. Archangel Zadkiel also works with the Violet Flame and with St Germain. And of course for the ultimate energy clearing top-off - call in Archangel Michael too. There are now further evolutions of the Violet Flame, such as the Cosmic Diamond Violet Flame, and the Gold, Silver and Violet Flame which you can work with.

Clearing the Energy of Places

Sometimes places, buildings, have stuck energy in them. For whatever reason, the energy can become dark and dense, affecting the people that come within the space according to how resilient and healthy their own energy is. People affect places, and places can also affect people. The good news is that we can clear the energy, and one way to do this is with Angels and Energy EFT.

You can work by proxy to do this. Try not to get too much into the energy of the story e.g. this happened there, and that happened there. If sad things happened there that you know about, it might be that other sad things happened way before that on the same land. There might be geopathic stress, or karma built up in its very foundations which you didn't know about. Which could be a factor in the events that were derived there afterwards. You don't need to know the whole story. The angels know all about it and they can deal with it. All you need to do is get the ball rolling with your intention and energy healing contributions.

<u>A Powerful Angel EFT Clearing Exercise for a place</u>

You may light a candle and dedicate it to the clearing, but a candle is not required.

Look at your open palms and mentally ask the angels to bless your healing hands with golden light.

Three deep breaths at heart centre. Complete this slowly and mindfully, taking the time to breathe and feel the energy between tapping points.

HC: Calling Archangel Michael, Archangel Zadkiel, St Germain and the Violet Flame to assist in clearing the energy of .... for the highest good of all

TH: Releasing any anxiety I have been holding about ....

TE: I surrender any fears I have about .... with the help of the angels now

EB: Inviting a clearing of my own energy when I think about ...... so that I may be a positive influence

SE: Inviting the Violet Flame to cleanse away any fears now that I may have held in my thoughts, in my words and in my energy field

UE: Thankyou Archangels' Michael and Zadkiel, and St Germain in assisting this clearing in me in relation to ......

UN: Now that I am clear I have made room for healing

(if you feel clear about sending healing to ..... then continue, if you are still holding onto fear or somehow stuck in the story, tap for longer on this. Use other techniques as needed, and if the place has very deep and disturbing associations for you work with an experienced Energy EFT practitioner before proceeding).

CH: I am now free to work with the angelic realms and beings of light to clear the energy of .....

CB: Sending a team of light and the Violet Flame to ..... now

Th: I open my heart and assist healing with my dedicated team of light

If: Thank you angels and St Germain for cleansing …. and all persons who think about this place with the mighty Violet Flame for the highest good of all
Mf: Thank you angels and St Germain for this powerful work
Rf: Thank you Violet Flame for serving ….. and those who are influenced by it
Bf: Thank you team of light for this powerful clearing
KC: Cleared, peaceful and healed for the highest good of all
Three deep breaths at heart centre
HC: Thank you for this powerful clearing, I trust that it is done, and I am free to detach now.

If you feel afterwards that the place in question could benefit from further clearing, you may repeat the above, using your own words. It can be that a place is cleared and healed, but energy may become somewhat clogged up again by people affected by the place. You can ask the angels to help those people too in relation to how their thoughts influence the energy of the place. Trust that your contributions have a massive effect, and are very worthwhile.

Planetary Healing with Angel EFT

Archangels Roquiel, Butyalil and Lady Gaia amongst others can be called upon in healing the planet. You should call upon the angels, but also if you are guided the Ascended Masters and elementals. You can use phrases such as:

Healing for the planet
Healthy, beautiful Earth
World Peace
Harmonious beautiful planet
Earth surrounded and infused with love
Love and compassion on Earth now
Peaceful healthy Earth
Angel healing for Earth
Oneness on Earth
Healthy energy on Earth

Chapter Summary:

● Proxy tapping – also called surrogate tapping - gives us the ability to help people and situations where teaching them to tap isn't an option.

● We can send healing to our own past aspects with Angel EFT proxy tapping, other people near and far, places, situations, animals and more.

● It's good to ask someone's permission first before sending them healing, but if for any reason this just isn't feasible we can ask the angels to divert the healing to someone or something nearby that wants it if the recipient doesn't want it.

● If you are sending healing to another person, place etc. remember to detach afterwards so that you don't form unhealthy cords with them.

● Dealing with the *aspect of our former self* when doing proxy work as opposed to our former self direct allows us to remain detached and free from abreactions in the case of stressful and traumatic past events.

● Archangel Fhelyai helps animals and is good to call upon when doing proxy work with animals.

● St Germain is the Ascended Master associated with the Violet Flame of purification and you can work with St Germain, Archangel Zadkiel and also Archangel Michael for purifying and clearing away negativity.

● Places can also benefit from energy work and clearing, as they can absorb negative energy.

● Proxy work can be very powerful in healing the planet, and you can call upon Archangel Butyalil, Archangel Roquiel and Lady Gaia amongst others to assist.

Chapter 11: Better Relationships

Our relationships are often like a mirror of how we are sometimes. And yet many of our relationships differ, so perhaps they mirror different facets of us. Our close relationships - that with our partner, children, closest friends may echo characteristics of our early relationships within the home. But first and foremost, our relationship with ourselves at this moment in time will influence all the rest. And because this is energy work, no matter what the psychology is behind how we are, we can change the energy of it and thus change our experiences. To cultivate improvements, call in the angels and get tapping.

In all of our relationships, we can rate them as they are in this moment on the SUE Scale, and ask the question 'what does this relationship need to move one point higher (or ten points higher)?

Relationship with Self

How we feel about ourselves, what we say about ourselves both aloud and in our head has a huge bearing on how we relate to others. I'm sure we have all heard it said that those who constantly gossip and put others down must be very unhappy with themselves? Well it's quite accurate. If we were feeling great in ourselves, we just wouldn't see all those faults in others. Or if we did they wouldn't bother us, as we are acting in a higher consciousness that has no concern in judging others but rather helping out. We can, quite literally, rise above all the pettiness.

If your relationship with yourself isn't so good, there are lots of things you can do to improve it.

 Ask yourself the following questions just now and write down your answers:

- *How much do I like myself right now in this moment?* Use the SUE Scale, i.e. minus ten is the least you can possibly like yourself and plus ten is the most you can possibly like yourself, zero means you feel indifference towards yourself.

- How much do I love myself right now in this moment?

- Are there things I would like to change in myself, and is the lack of these changes affecting the way I feel about myself?

- Am I angry or fed up with myself about something? If so, what is it? Write down the thing or things.

If you are not happy with yourself, why not? And who might be upset if you were happy and loving towards yourself from here on? What would this look like on the high positives of the SUE Scale? How would it change and transform?

Now call in the angels and do some tapping. Archangel Uriel can help you to heal old resentments towards the self and release fear which is what we are carrying when we are at odds with the self. You can create your own rounds which will be much more specific and deal with one thing at a time if this is complex for you, but this round offers a start, generally for increasing self-love and forgiveness. If you carry a lot of resentment towards yourself, persistence will pay.

Visualisation: Close your eyes and take your attention to the soles of your feet. Ground yourself. Breathe a few comfortable breaths and call in your own guardian angel, who is always willing to help you heal your relationships. Feel your angels' wings wrap around you keeping you in a cocoon of light. Feel a stream of golden light washing down over you, bathing your energy and the physical body in love and light.

Now call in Archangel Uriel. Feel his beautiful golden sunny energy around you now. Breathe a few deep cleansing, relaxing breaths. Tell Archangel Uriel of your intention to improve your relationship with yourself, for the highest good of all. Notice any sensations or messages. Now in your mind's eye tune into your relationship with yourself. As though it is an energy in your body. Where is it? What colour or shape is it? What is it doing, and what is it like? What does it need? Breathe into it. See Archangel Uriel sending healing light to it now.

Now place your hands on the heart centre.

Three deep breaths.

HC: Archangel Uriel I would like to have a wonderful, happy and peaceful relationship with myself

TH: For the highest good of all

TE: I know that by loving myself I have more love to give to others

EB: There are things about me that I get annoyed about

SE: Things that I regret and wish I could have done differently

UE: I ask for forgiveness from the deepest part of my being now

UN: Witnessed by my angels and my higher self

CH: I release any ideas I may have been holding in my being about not being able to love myself

CB: I release with love and respect any ancestral heritage that may have brought about any unhelpful beliefs or energies

Th: Me loving myself is beneficial to all

If: Thank you Archangel Uriel for clearing away any fear from my being, now, about me

Mf: And replacing it with pure love and light

Rf: I am now choosing to have a good relationship with me

Bf: To love, honour and stand by myself

KC: I am open to your guidance and wisdom now so that I may carry this work forward

HC: Creating new healthy patterns in my relationship with myself now

Tune in again and see if that energy is still there and what it is like now. Draw or write down anything you would like to remember. If you have had a troublesome relationship with yourself for years, keep going. Make a point of doing this regularly for as long as you need. Take a curious interest in the changes that occur.

The Power of Giving and Receiving

Funny enough, I have met many healers and light workers that are kind hearted people, but that put themselves last in quite a self-destructive way. They find it hard to accept money for the work they do, they have poor boundaries with others and are frequently let down, taken advantage of and even bullied. Still they continue to give and give and give, and end up depleted and frequently burned out. This is indicative of a poor relationship with self. Having healthy boundaries, taking good care of yourself, accepting money, favours, gifts etc are all a sign of a good relationship with the self.

Giving all the time is a male dominant energy and receiving is female (nothing to do with gender but rather the energy). If you give all the time, or receive all the time without doing the other your energies become unbalanced. Accepting a compliment, even if you don't really agree with it, is one way of exercising your receiving energy. Look the person in the eye and say 'thank you.' Some people find that tricky. If you care for people and aren't often given things, give to yourself. Acts of kindness to the self don't need to be very expensive or time-consuming. Just make a point, even if you are buying yourself a pair of socks, or taking a nice walk, say to yourself 'this is a gift to me.'

Relationship with Partner

This section is aimed at people in a relationship which might not be feeling too great, but you'd love for it to be going better. There exists an energy between you and your partner, imagine it for a moment as a tube that connects you, I remember Sai Maa Lakshmi Devi describing it something like this. What is in the tube is what you put in and what they put in. What you both bring to the relationship. So the quality of what is in the tube is dependent on you both, but you are only responsible for what you put in.

So using your energy mind close your eyes now and see what it looks like in the tube. Ask your angel to light it up for you to see. Observe, without judgement, what is going on in there. It's all only energy! And we know that we can change the energy of things with our intention if we so wish. The angels have an amazing way of guiding us to what we need; sometimes it might be a new way of communicating, to a course, book or therapist.

Angel EFT to bring more love into the relationship with your partner

Three deep breaths at heart centre

HC: Archangel Chamuel assist me now in bringing more love into my relationship with ....

TH: I am open to releasing any unhealthy patterns in my being that I have brought into my relationship

TE: I open my heart now to more love for myself and for my partner

EB: I release any hurts or fears that have been holding me back in my relationship

SE: Releasing any old beliefs that have been hanging around in my being

UE: That may have been holding me back

UN: I would *love* to experience more love in my relationship

CH: Love and romance

CB: Love and fun

Th: Love and divine bliss

If: Thank you Archangel Chamuel for helping me to heal any heart issues now

Mf: So that I may experience the best relationship possible with ....

Rf: I love to be in love

Bf: I give myself permission to give and receive love

KC: I am open to angelic guidance and wisdom

HC: Thank you for my wonderful relationship with ....

Tune in again and have a look at the tube, how is it now? What does it need?
You can of course tap on much more specific issues within your relationship. Maybe there was an incident that you resent, and tapping for the former aspect of yourself by proxy with the angels would help to free up the energy of resentment. You can tap for a better sex life, for more quality time together, for

healthier lifestyles together, fun and exciting opportunities, new home etc. You can address an Archangel of your choice or the angels of love and fun, for example. Keep going.

Relationship with Children

It's funny how some people say it's easier to spend time with their niece than their daughter, even though naturally they love their daughter the most. The energy is clearer between the aunty and the niece, whereas the energy between mother and daughter (or mother and son, father-daughter etc.) has a much busier, complex energy. Imagine the tube again, described in Relationship with Partner section, and check in how the tube is looking between you and one of your children. The parent child relationship is often full of stories.

From the worried parent you could have:

I never spend enough time with you and this makes me feel bad; I let you stay up too late and too much time gaming and I feel like a bad parent; you are cheeky to me; I never would have spoken to my parents the way you speak to me; I love you so much I wish I knew how to show it; I wish you could do better at school I want you to have good opportunities in the future.

From the child you could have:

I wish you spent more time with me, you are always busy; I feel as though you don't care sometimes; I think you compare me to ……. who always does well at school; I feel like I am a disappointment; I'd like if you appreciated my achievements and show an interest in me.

Archangel Gabriel is good to call upon in the case of children, but also Archangel Raguel especially in resolving conflict.

General round for parenting:

Three deep breaths at heart centre
HC: Archangel Gabriel I want to be the best parent that I can be
TH: I find it really hard sometimes
TE: They didn't come with an instruction manual
EB: And sometimes me doing my best doesn't feel up to scratch
SE: I'd love to let go of any regrets I'm hanging on to
UE: I know it doesn't benefit ………….. (name of child or children)
UN: I am open to the knowing that I am a good enough parent
CH: I don't need to get it right all of the time
CB: But I'm happy to do my very best with your help and love
Th: Releasing any old stuff from my own childhood now that might have been holding me back
If: Freeing me up in my relationship with …………
Mf: Happy peaceful parenting
Rf: Peaceful and calm and loving
Bf: Loving towards myself and my child(ren)
KC: thank you Archangel Gabriel for your guidance and wisdom
HC: I open up to the wisdom now and radiate peace and calm for my child(ren)

What else does this relationship need to really flourish? Tap on the positives.

Visualise: See yourself radiating peace and calm. Your children can't help but pick up on it. When you treat yourself with kindness your children learn to do likewise. Stay with eyes closed for a moment. Imagine your child or children in turn, with their guardian angel behind them, enfolding them with their wings. See how loved they are. Imagine them enveloped in peace and love. Ask Archangel Gabriel for any further wisdom or insights that will help you in your relationship with your children.

Other Family Members

Use this also for in-laws / friends / colleagues or people you know and with whom you'd like to improve the relationship.

Pick a relationship within the family (or other) that you would like to bring more positive energy into. Just one at a time is best, but we can do a round also for family in general. Remember that what you experience is in part a mirror of something going on in you. But I hear people say in cases of conflict 'no it's all him/her, everyone says it, they run into trouble wherever they go.' If that is the case, why is it bothering you? If you work on raising your frequency you can rise above it and they won't upset you. This is not said to make people feel as though every conflict in their life is their own fault, rather to empower you to take the reins. When we spend our time blaming and accusing others we don't feel empowered, rather like a hapless victim being blown here and there.

So imagine this person and yourself, and the tube which is the relationship between you. What is in there? Ask your angels to light it up so you can see. Take some deep breaths and ask Archangel Chamuel to fill your heart up with love and compassion. If you feel very resentful towards this person it may help to visualise them as a tiny baby, just arrived here on earth at the very start of their journey with their guardian angel beside them. Feel your heart soften as the angels fill it with even more love. Now bring the picture back to your mind of the tube, and ask what is needed for a better relationship with this person. Notice your thoughts. Are they full of drama and stories, or are they raised up into your higher mind, where you feel in touch with wisdom and calm? If the former, ask for more peace and calm, for the highest good of all concerned. Call upon Archangel Raguel and Archangel Michael to assist you now in this relationship.

Angel EFT to heal a relationship

Three deep breaths at heart centre

HC: Archangel Raguel please assist me in my relationship with......

TH: I would like more love and light in this relationship now

TE: I am open to releasing any resentments or any ego stuff on my part that has been getting in the way

EB: I would like to be a positive influence in my relationship with ....

SE: I detach from any drama now, no matter how entangled I might have felt in it in the past

UE: I am free to be responsible for my part in this relationship now

UN: I would like to rise above any lower frequency energies

CH: And to focus on compassion and love

CB: Letting go of any cords of fear I may have experienced with this person

Th: Archangel Michael please cut any cords now

If: And I accept pure love and light in the place of any cords or fear based energy

Mf: Healing this relationship in all directions of time

Rf: Sending the pure love and light of the angels to ....

Bf: Allowing room for cooperation and all the good things that are possible

KC: Happy, peaceful relationship with ....

HC: Thank you for my happy, peaceful relationship with ....

Visualise yourself and the other person and add even more light to the tube now. Write down any messages or insights and continue to tap as needed.

Phone calls

Sometimes making an important call can feel like a big ordeal, but tapping and calling in the angels before you do can really help. Check in how you are feeling right now about making that call. How do you measure on the SUE Scale? If you are in the minuses, chances are you need to start with de-stressing yourself. Choose a positive word or focus and an angel or Archangel.

Three deep breaths at heart centre

HC: Archangel Michael grant me the courage to make this call with confidence

TH: Confidence on the call

TE: Feeling positive and assertive

EB: Open to the possibility of assistance for the highest good of all concerned

SE: Attracting the best possible outcome

UE: I trust that the angels know what's best

UN: They can see things that I can't see

CH: Calm and confident that all is well

CB: And I trust that they will assist me in making this call and what comes of it

Th: Thank you Archangel Michael

If: Thank you for this calm and confident feeling

Mf: The energy of confidence is flowing over me now

Rf: I send blessings to …….. (the person at the other end of the phone)

Bf: I am grateful for this calm and confident feeling

KC: Calm and self-assured

HC: Thank you Archangel Michael

Chapter Summary:

● Our relationships can mirror a part of ourselves and we can learn from them and evolve using energy healing and asking the angels.

● Our relationship with ourselves affects all of our other relationships.

● Giving is the masculine energy and receiving is the feminine, and we need to be able to do both regularly for good health and well-being.

● You can imagine that you are connected by a tube to the other person you are in a relationship with. You both contribute to and affect what's in the tube. We bring our stuff from the past to the relationship, and can with intention heal past beliefs, behaviours and patterns.

● Our relationships with our children is helped by Archangel Gabriel, and we can help purify and release the unhelpful stories that clutter it up, and help ourselves to feel like a good enough parent which in turn helps our child.

● Archangel Raguel can help with relationships especially where there has been conflict.

● If we take responsibility in all of our relationships, we can facilitate positive changes.

Chapter 12: Dealing with Low Mood

I included this chapter as an acknowledgement of gratitude to all the people I have worked with who have suffered from depression, in my nursing and counselling and in day to day life. I learned so much from them. But also to those who suffer from sporadic low mood - probably every human on the planet since it is part of the human condition. From my own personal experience also, I will share the techniques I have used that have worked.

Depression itself is diagnosed by a doctor and sometimes treated with medication, and sometimes not. I will talk here about low mood, whether as a symptom of depression or low mood in its own right. It has different depths, different levels of severity. Like in the case of an auto-immune disease the body is attacking itself, in low mood it is sometimes as though the mind attacks itself with negative self-depreciating thoughts. Which, if entertained only make things worse. By entertained I mean believed, and encouraged, which is usually done unwittingly. In recovering from lows, we either sail naturally past the doom and gloom thoughts, or we have to cleverly reframe our thinking. We learn to answer those thoughts back, and correct them.

Low mood shows up on the SUE Scale typically anything from -2 to -10 being the most severe.

 If you are feeling so low that you have thoughts of harming yourself or ending your life you need to go and get help right away.

Angels and Low Mood

Of course the angels don't leave us because our mood is low, but it may be harder to accept that they are there. Harder to feel them and sense them. Your guardian angel is always with you and will support you indefinitely, and even more so when you ask. For those who have called more angels into their lives, either themselves or by others' prayers and intentions there will be more alongside the guardian angel, ushering in support.

 When we feel low we should ask the question *where do I feel this in my body?* Is it in the heart? Is it in the head? The stomach?

Having the awareness of where the sadness or heartache is gives us an opening for awareness and energy healing. Greif is felt in the heart. People can literally feel as though their heart is broken. Others describe low mood as a fuzziness or dullness in their head, or a sinking feeling in the stomach. What colour, shape or texture is it?

We can call in whatever Archangels we feel guided to. Calling in Archangel Chamuel for the heart, Jophiel for the head and Uriel for the solar plexus may be a useful start if you are unsure. I also believe that people with low mood often have cords to cut and so asking Archangel Michael to scan and cut those cords will help to free up the energy as much as possible. Archangel Zadkiel can bring in the Violet Flame to heal and purify the thoughts and energy.

The Voice of Depression

Depression has a voice. It is not your voice although you may think it is. Depression says:
I am no good
I have never been any good
Life is always hard
Things aren't going to get any better
They don't like me   ....And so on

To counteract the voice of depression acknowledge it for what it is. Say 'I hear the voice of depression talking again. I can take it on board or I can answer it back. My choice. I know when I take it on board I feel worse.'

You can counteract the voice of depression by using affirmations. Make your own, but a few ideas could be:

- My mood is getting better and better

- I breathe in light and peace

- I am loved and protected by my angels always

- There are many wonderful opportunities coming up in my life

The 'So I need to'...Technique

Another technique I like to use is to follow up a negative thought with the words 'so I need to....' For example, if you hear your thoughts saying 'oh, I feel so miserable,' follow it up with the words 'so I need to...' and listen to what follows. 'oh I feel so miserable' on its own affirms and strengthens the fact that you are feeling miserable. But when you say 'so I need to..' you are inviting solution-focused thinking.

Believe it or not we all have the answers to our own problems. Yes, we may look to others, learn from books, professionals, role models etc and learn from them but if you stop and think about what might make you feel better right now you have the answers. If it's hard to think about it like that, reframe it as though a good friend was telling you they felt miserable. What might you advise them to do to feel better?

Mood Raising Tips

✓ Move. Dance. Exercise. Research has shown that exercising regularly is believed to be at least as effective as antidepressant medication in helping heal depression.

✓ Plant something and nurture it, watch it grow.

✓ Get outdoors. If it's cold and rainy dress accordingly, but getting out is important.

✓ Look at beautiful things, if there isn't much beauty around get some nice pictures, for something quick look for beautiful images on the web.

✓ Do something nice and nurturing for yourself, it doesn't have to be expensive. Soaking your feet is one example.

✓ Sprinkle two or three drops of lavender essential oil on your pillow a few hours before you go to bed.

✓ Gratitude – this is useful in so many areas of life but in fighting negative thoughts you could start to answer them back with 'but I feel so grateful that....'

✓ Avoid Toxins: Give your body and head the best chance by choosing healthy foods and beverages.

✓ Write out a do-able to-do list each day and try your best to stick to it. In the case of being actually depressed, keep it to the bare but important essentials: eat, shower, walk and whatever else you can manage that you need to do and is likely to make you feel better.

✓ Spend time with animals.

Guilt and Shame

Shame is one of the most destructive emotions we can have. Guilt is feeling bad about something you did or didn't do whereas shame is feeling bad about yourself as a person. Shame is harder to reach since it is not about a specific event, although specific events may trigger it. It has been there longer. If you carry shame it is worth working thoroughly on releasing it as it will hold you back time and time again. It often carries along generations. A child unconsciously picks up their mother, grandfather, aunts shame without ever knowing it. See Chapter 7 for healing ancestral patterns.

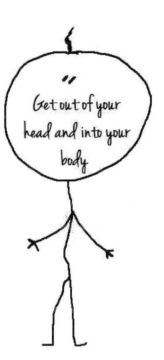

If you have shame or guilt, get used to listening out to what your thoughts say. Feel free to question them, cross examine them to get to the heart of the matter. Talk back to your thoughts just as you might talk to a friend who was telling you they feel guilty or ashamed about something. Don't allow the thoughts to just run freely. To feel better and stay better, you must challenge them.

Ask the questions to know what to tap for

Tapping on feeling so depressed is too global, and is *stress talk* anyway, so we need to break it down into specifics. If you are low, ask the questions:

What does low mean to me?
Where is low in my body?
If low had a voice what would it say?
If low had a colour and shape what would that be?

If there are specific upsets connected with 'low' work on them individually.

If you are very low, consistently low or diagnosed with having depression it's advisable to work with a skilled practitioner, in particular someone trained in mental health.

Not feeling worthy of help or not motivated to help ourselves

When people have low mood they may feel that they don't deserve to feel better or to have the things they dream about. Anger turned in on the self, resentment towards self and others are sometimes part of the toxic cocktail that is depression.

Tapping for feeling worthy and motivated to help ourselves

HC: I don't know that I deserve to feel good
TH: Angels help me to do the best I can
TE: Even though I'm not sure that I am worthy
EB: All this resentment
SE: It's so heavy to carry
UE: I don't know how to put it down
UN: But I am choosing to do the best I can anyway
CH: The best I can manage in this moment
CB: I'd like to feel a little more worthy
Th: I can support myself in feeling a little more motivated
If: I mightn't be able to change much today
Mf: But I am willing to help myself a little bit

Rf: Thank you angels for helping me even when I don't feel worthy
Bf: Thank you for your support
KC: I am open to moving forward just a little bit right now

Sabotage

We sabotage ourselves because we want to feel safe. It sounds strange I know, but people can be more afraid of health than ill-health, of success than of failure. That which is familiar feels safe, even if it's problematic. Sabotage certainly doesn't just affect us when we have low mood, and this round could be adapted to use for sabotage in other areas. However, there is a part of depression that echoes sabotage in terms of deserving.

Round for sabotage in helping yourself to recover from low mood

Three deep breaths at heart centre
HC: Angels I have noticed that I tend to sabotage
TH: Then I get so annoyed with myself
TE: Why do I do this?
EB: I'd really love your help with this
SE: Because a big part of me really wants to move forward and feel good
UE: I'd really love to do things that I know help me to feel good
UN: Sabotage is so familiar
CH: And there's that part of me that just wants to feel safe
CB: Safe in the status quo
Th: I'm allowing myself to be calm
If: And I'm open to your guidance on this one angels
Mf: I know you can help me when I ask
Rf: I'd like some insight on my reasons for sabotaging this
Bf: So that I can heal what it is that needs healing
KC: I'd love to move forward and feel safe to do so
HC: Thank you angels for your support and insights

<u>I know tapping works but I'm not doing it</u>

I hear this so often, why not try a de-stress round first and then:

HC: Tapping has helped before but I just don't feel like it

TH: Angels help me to clear any resistance

TE: I don't really want to stay stuck

EB: I'd like to do something positive and help myself

SE: I don't feel like tapping sometimes

UE: It might be that sometimes I'm afraid of moving forward

UN: And I'm not going to force myself into anything outside of my comfort zone

CH: Angels help me to release any self-worth stuff that may be getting in my way

CB: Nobody else truly benefits from me being stuck

Th: I release some of my resistance now

If: I'm allowed to hold on to some of it if that's what I really want right now

Mf: It's okay for me to not let go of all of it in one go

Rf: I might feel too threatened by that just now

Bf: And I just want to feel safe

KC: Safe and loved

HC: So even if I don't feel like it I commit to supporting myself anyway

<u>Clutter and Overwhelm</u>

Cluttering the living space, the car, the schedule or the head can take its toll on our mood. All types of clutter are linked to our energy and emotions. Similarly, someone in a low mood can find themselves in a cluttered environment, it might feel too much to tidy up. People hold onto things 'just in case I might need it someday,' or 'just in case I'll regret throwing it away,' and end up with too much stuff and a sense of overwhelm. Overwhelm can in turn lead to low mood. In Chapter 3 I include a round working with Archangel Jophiel for the crown chakra and for making the home beautiful. Also in Chapter 10 I include working to clear the energy of a place with Archangel Michael, Archangel Zadkiel and the Violet Flame. This powerful round can also be good in preparation for de-cluttering.

Overwhelm and de-cluttering:

Three deep breaths at heart centre
HC: I feel so overwhelmed
TH: I don't know where to start
TE: Archangel Zadkiel please help in raising the energy and purifying clutter
EB: I allow for my own energy to be cleansed and cleared now
SE: I notice my resistance to dealing with this
UE: And I choose to support myself
UN: Rome wasn't built in a day
CH: But it did get built
CB: One step at a time
Th: I choose to take the first step
If: To do things that support me in clearing my energy and the space I live in
Mf: I want to feel good about …….. (whatever it is you want to declutter)
Rf: I support myself in taking one step at a time
Bf: Thank you Archangel Zadkiel for your help in purifying
KC: I know we can work together on this
HC: Thank you my loving guardian angel for helping to energise me to take action

What other positives would help you to progress further now? Keep tapping, finish at HC with 'thank you Archangel Zadkiel and guardian angel.'

Chapter Summary

- Low mood is experienced by all human beings at some point in their life. It may be a symptom of depression or just a mind state in its own right. It shows up on the SUE Scale from about -2 to -10.

- Low mood is exacerbated by negative thoughts which if left unchallenged make it worse.

- If we tune into where we feel the low feeling in the body it can guide us to which Archangel we might like to call upon, although of course it's fine to ask any angel or Archangel you like to work with.

- Cord cutting with Archangel Michael and working with Archangel Zadkiel and the Violet Flame to purify can help heal the negative energy associated with depression.

- The 'voice of depression' is always negative. It is good to learn to recognise the voice of depression and to challenge it. Affirmations can help in answering back depression.

- Regular exercise is thought to be at least as effective as antidepressant medication.

- Getting outdoors, gardening, spending time with animals, doing something nurturing for the self, avoiding toxins in the diet, using essential oils such as lavender, making a realistic to-do list to focus yourself are some of the things that you can do to help raise the mood.

- Gratitude puts your focus on the things you appreciate in life and trains the mind away from low mood thoughts.

- Shame is one of the most destructive emotions and can pass on from one generation to the next. Overcoming shame is a huge step in personal development and keeping the mood good.

- Questioning thoughts instead of letting them run on auto-pilot is a useful strategy in re-training the mind.

- Break tapping rounds down into specifics, 'I feel so depressed' is too global. Ask where the feeling is in the body or break it down into specific feelings or worries and tap on each one at a time.

- Not feeling worthy or motivated, sabotaging and not tapping even though it helps are all tappable issues.

- Overwhelm and cluttering can contribute to low mood and likewise clearing these can help us to overcome low mood and feel really good.

Chapter 13: Manifesting Abundance

<u>Be Clear about What You Want</u>

Abundance can mean getting more money, but it can be a much more ambiguous concept than that: having lots of lovely things in your life. The word abundance means 'a very large quantity of something.' I suggest in doing abundance work getting clear about what the *something* is that you want a very large quantity of. Exquisite things such as love, a devoted relationship, family time, holidays, time out, exotic food, a healthy looking savings account.

Not being clear is another block to abundance. It leads to inertia, procrastination and other sabotaging behaviours. Whatever it is that you'd like, be sure about it. And perhaps look at one thing at a time. The angels can help as always. So in this first round I'll address that issue of clarity.

Tapping for clarity with Archangel Gabriel

Three deep breaths at heart centre
HC: Archangel Gabriel I want to be really clear now
TH: Please help me to get clear about what I want
TE: I choose to release anything that gets in the way of me being clear
EB: I allow myself to easily make decisions
SE: To intuitively know what is good for me
UE: The things that match up with what I am working towards
UN: I release any unhelpful patterns now
CH: Patterns of me not being clear about what I want
CB: Thank you Archangel Gabriel
Th: I know you can see things about me and what is good for me
If: I am open to your loving guidance

Mf: I choose to relax and tune in so that I can get clear
Rf: So that I can attract the things I want
Bf: And take positive action
KC: Thank you for this clarity
HC: I am open to your guidance and allow myself to be focussed

What do you need to be even more clear? What positive energy would benefit you? Keep tapping.

Allow yourself some time afterwards with eyes closed. Make pictures in your mind's eye about the things you would like. Make the picture really strong, really detailed. If any resistance surfaces, any arguments, simply make a mental note of them. You can work on them afterwards.

Seeking out Blocks and Working Through Them

The other really important thing in abundance and manifestation work is to become aware of any blocks you have, and weed them out with Angel EFT. As you read through these if some are applicable to you, think about their corresponding opposite. How do they rate on the SUE Scale for you and what is the positive opposite of that limiting belief? Write that down as it gives you something to tap on, and an affirmation.

Some of the kind of blocks to financial abundance people get:

• An underlying belief of not deserving good things
• A family pattern of not-having, and so subscribing to the family code (unconsciously)
• Messages from childhood or media that rich people are bad, materialistic, money makes you immoral and selfish, if you had money you'd be hounded etc.
• 'I can't handle money' fears
• 'Money just slips through my fingers' thoughts
• Feelings of inferiority or being less than others

- I got money before and lost it all
- My parents had money and lost it all
- If I had money I would turn into…. (an alcoholic, a gambling addict, a power hungry fanatic, a kleptomaniac … etc)
- If I had money my partner might not love me anymore, or, my marriage would fail
- If I had money somebody else would suffer
- I might not be the caring, giving person any more, it might change who I am
- My friends/family would be jealous

… and so it goes on. If you think you have any such blocks note these down as they are the first most important step in your abundance journey.

 If you don't know if you have any, first ask yourself *'how safe would I feel if I could have ………… right this minute?'* If the answer is completely safe but yet it's been so far really hard to manifest this thing you could tap to reveal any specific blocks.

See also Case Example of Steven in Chapter 3.

Tapping for revealing blocks to abundance with Archangel Raziel

Three deep breaths at heart centre
HC: Archangel Raziel please help me to see any blocks I have to abundance
TH: Any old beliefs that have been holding me back
TE: I choose to find out what they are so I can heal them
EB: Raising my consciousness to a higher level
SE: Letting go of old limiting patterns that have stopped me from manifesting
UE: The things that I want
UN: Thank you Archangel Raziel
CB: For helping me to manifest
Th: For clearing the way so I can attract what I want
If: I trust in your guidance and support
Mf: I allow my subconscious mind to show me now

Rf: Any abundance blocks so that I may release them
Bf: Thank you for this help
KC: I choose to be confidently insightful
HC: Making way for clear manifestation now
Finish with a few minutes' stillness with eyes closed, tuning in to whatever comes up. Make a note of ideas and revelations, and repeat if necessary. This is really valuable material for you in moving your abundance forward.

 Sometimes when doing abundance work people can end up on a very long-winded 'treasure hunt' as the block-finding leads from one thing to another. I suggest making every second round a very focused positive round, so that if you are working on your abundance this is what you stay working on.

A very general round for abundance might be simply saying angels of abundance on each tapping point, or you could call in Archangels Ariel, Raphael and Raziel and tap on their names and the word 'easily attracting money/abundance/sun holiday.' Alternatively, a round such as this one:

Three deep breaths at heart centre
HC: Angels of Abundance I would like to manifest ……………….. by …………….. with your loving assistance if this is for my highest good
TH: Archangel Raphael assist me to clarify my vision now of what I want
TE: Clear my third eye of any debris so that I am free to manifest with clear pictures of what I want in my mind
EB: Archangels Ariel and Raziel please assist me in manifesting ………………..
SE: I trust in your loving guidance to attract wonderful new opportunities into my life
UE: Manifesting ……………………………………..

174

UN: .... coming into my life now

CH: I safely and powerfully manifest that which is good for me

CB: Releasing any fears and doubts now and making way for .... to come into my life

Th: Seeing myself having .... in my life and feeling so joyous

If: Having this very clear image of me rejoicing now that this is in my life

Mf: Thank you Archangel Raphael

Rf: Thank you Archangel Ariel

Bf: Thank you Archangel Raziel

KC: Thank you for your guidance and love

HC: Angels of Abundance thank you for your ongoing assistance

Futuristic Tapping

I also have a technique that I love using whereby I tap as though I am in the future and have already manifested whatever it is, so 'angels I am so happy and grateful now that it is the 6th of March …. and I have this in my life.' It is so uplifting and exciting to do this, and puts you in the energy of what it feels like to have manifested what it is that you want.

For my Highest Good

When you work with the angels and the law of attraction you can ask as well that you manifest that which is for your highest good. We can't always see what the angels can see. An example was me going for a job interview some years ago. Thinking that this job was meant for me and I would surely get it - there were only two of us going for it, and I had a really clear vision in my mind. I did all the things I could to *line up* and attract this job.

Driving into town for the interview I even saw my very first angel in the clouds. I'd heard about these angel shaped clouds and always wanted to see one. I said to myself, 'it's a sign from the angels; I'm definitely going to get it.' The interview went well I thought, and I was shocked to learn some days later that the other candidate had got the job. *What?* How could that be? I was upset, couldn't understand it. I was sure it was meant for me, even though I knew that the other candidate was a good fit for the job.

Two weeks later the guy who got the job told me he had had to resign. That the job wasn't what he had imagined, and involved a lot of unexpected long distance travelling and was extremely stressful. I didn't know all this when I was preparing for my interview. I had mistakenly believed that the job was destined for me, had my name on it, and that it was fabulous. Luckily for me I didn't get it. It just showed me how, yes, the angels are supporting me. And they know more than I do, and that includes what is for my highest good.

So if you like you can include in your rounds, 'if this is for my highest good,' or 'this, or better please angels.'

<u>Support Your Vision, surround yourself in reminders</u>

I work with vision boards which is like a collage made either by sticking pictures onto a large sheet of card or creating it on a computer - of all the things you'd like to attract into your life. I do the latter and I print them off and keep them in view, but also use them as desktop background and on my phone lock screen. It's constantly visible. Of course you can update the vision board if things change, but do keep note of what you have manifested so that you can see your progress and encourage gratitude which is an abundance magnet. I do this by making a *thankyou board* also, which has all of that which I have already manifested and am grateful for.

The law of attraction states that our experiences are a result of our thoughts. It is not the only law, and other forces are at play. But the teaching has for me been extremely useful. If my thoughts affect my experiences, then what can I do to improve things? It gives us back some responsibility and empowers us to make changes we never thought possible.

 How many times has it rung true for you? Examples of the law of attraction in action include:

- You are afraid you will put on weight and you do

- You are confident you'll pass the test and you do

- You think you won't be believed or taken seriously and you are not

- You visualise yourself on that special holiday and by some way, somehow, you get there

- You are afraid you will drop something and you do

- You believe you will get an angel sign and you get one

- You say 'I never have any time,' and you don't

- You see that parking space in your mind before you get there, and there it is!

All the time our thoughts are influencing our experience. This frightens some people. But fear not, the energy it takes to have that negative thought is just as easily spent on a positive thought. Some of us grew up around worrisome, negative thinking parents, who probably in turn grew up around them too. But it's never too late to adopt a new way of thinking. Think of 'thought hygiene,' if you will, and catch yourself when you have a worrisome or negative thought.

My thoughts

Make a list now of your own worrisome or negative thoughts. Without judgement, and if you are used to law of attraction work it's possible you won't have many, but be vigilant, look thoroughly. There could be some tucked away somewhere. If you are having trouble finding any say the following affirmations out loud to yourself and note how they true they are for you just now (and how they show up on the SUE Scale):

- Money comes to me easily

- My relationships are all in perfect harmony

- I deeply love and appreciate my body

- My home is beautiful and bright

Affirmations are a powerful tool to help us manifest things in our life and work best when repeated over and over on a regular basis. But again as discussed in Chapter 9, they also work to show up doubts that we have and conflict. If we have this we can either keep saying the affirmation and hope that after time we start to believe it – this works sometimes, particularly if we use Positive EFT. Otherwise look at the thoughts that come up and work with the energy of these.

Examples of thoughts and related energies/physical symptoms:

Affirmation	Contradicting Thought	Possible energy and physical symptom
Money comes to me easily	It doesn't, I'm always struggling	Tight feeling in head, muddy third eye chakra
My relationships are all in perfect harmony	I'm always fighting with …… so they aren't in harmony really	Angry dark feeling in throat, constricted heart chakra
I deeply love and appreciate my body	I don't like the way my body looks, I wish I was in better shape	Heavy feeling in chest, sacral chakra issues
My home is beautiful and bright	My home is a mess I can never keep on top of it	Base chakra congestion, crushing feeling in shoulders

So for the first one you could tap for 'tight feeling in my head' or do some third eye chakra work, tied in with Archangel Raphael and having a clear vision of you attracting money.

Chapter Summary:

● Being clear about what it is you want to attract is the first step in manifesting. Asking for abundance is vague. What is abundance to you?

● If you have been trying to manifest something and it is not happening, seek out the blocks and systematically clear them.

● When looking for and dealing with blocks to abundance remember to intersperse with highly focused positive rounds, so as not to get lost or lose sight of what you want to attract.

● Ask the angels to help you manifest that which is for your highest good. We can't always see what is for our highest good, and sometimes we don't manifest something because it is not for us or there is something better.

● Surround yourself in reminders of what you want to manifest. Have a clear vision in your mind and use things like vision boards and images to keep your focus close by.

● Become mindful of thoughts which attract and repel what you desire.

● Use affirmations to manifest and also to reveal resistance that you can then work on. Look at what is happening in the energy body and use Angel EFT to work through it.

Chapter 14: Ascension Work - The Twelve Fifth Dimensional Chakras

Ascension work is about raising our vibration to the point of light. It is *not* about suddenly bursting into white flames or floating off to the heavens, unless that is our prerogative of course. It involves purifying and clearing our emotions and thoughts, and our actions come from love, for the highest good. We radiate at a higher level which is joyous and free. This is us in the fifth dimension. In the third dimension we struggle and life is hard. Fourth dimension, as mentioned earlier is somewhere in between.

For those who are new to the chakras, it is best to familiarise yourself with the 7 third dimensional chakras first, and complete those exercises. This chapter is likely to appeal to those who are used to working with energy, angels, Ascended Masters, meditation and the chakras. I learned about these chakras in 2012 from the Diana Cooper Foundation, and they appear in Diana Cooper's books and are available in a DVD format. The earlier version I learned also had physical exercises and breathing exercises, toning and visualising the petals of the chakras opening and closing.

Read these exercises through fully first before doing them, so that you know what they are about and you know that this resonates with you. Do them as a continuous flow, one after the other. I haven't included symbols for de-stressing, re-wording, repeating or SUE Scale this time. I have also suggested different *pre* set-up points for each chakra, instead of three breaths at the heart centre. For this work stand with your feet hip width apart if this is comfortable otherwise try to sit with your spine straight feet flat on the floor. The energy is heightened working with these chakras and when I do them I stand but often keep a chair to hand in case I need to sit down. These are best done all together one after the other.

The Antakarana, mentioned in the stellar gateway chakra Angel EFT round, is an Indian term depicting a bridge of light between soul and vessel.

To prepare, light a candle, ask the angels to clear and cleanse the space you are working in. Call in Archangel Michael to protect your energy and the space, and remove any lower frequency energies. Ask the angels to bless your healing hands with golden light. Angel cards and crystals would be a nice accompaniment if you have these, but are not essential.

<u>Earth Star Chakra</u>

The earth star chakra is twelve inches below your feet, and the colour is black and white. Archangels Roquiel and Sandalphon assist in integrating this chakra, which helps us to be fully grounded and brings spirit into matter.

Angel EFT to activate and integrate the fifth dimensional Earth Star chakra

Visualise: Be aware of the soles of your feet, and down to a point twelve inches below your feet. Feel the energy passing from one sole, down to the earth star chakra, back to the other sole, and then back across to the first foot creating a triangle of energy. See Archangels Roquiel and Sandalphon place a ball of black and white energy into your earth star chakra.

Take three deep breaths with hands by your sides. Have you palms facing downwards if you are sitting.

HC: Archangels Roquiel and Sandalphon please assist me in activating and integrating my earth star chakra
TH: I allow this light to anchor in my being now
TE: *Breathe comfortable full breaths as you feel the energy integrate*
EB: *No need to talk, just breathe comfortable full breaths*
SE: Thank you for helping me to assimilate spirit into matter
UE: *Breathe a comfortable full breath as you feel the energy integrate*
UN: *Keep breathing comfortable, full breaths*
CH: I tune into who I truly am and my immense capability here on this planet

CB: I feel the connection between me and Mother Earth

Th: I am deeply grounded on this planet and in my being

If: Thank you Archangels Roquiel and Sandalphon for allowing me to know any new learning from my earth star chakra today

Mf: *No talking just breathe comfortable full breath as you feel the energy integrate*

Rf: *No talking just breathe comfortable full breath*

Bf: I choose to nurture my potential

KC: Thank you Archangels Roquiel and Sandalphon for my activated earth star chakra

HC: I am loved and blessed

Pause to allow the new energy to settle

Base Chakra

The base chakra is at the base of the spine radiating down, and the colour is platinum. Archangel Gabriel assists in integrating this chakra, which helps you to trust that the universe supports you and you will always be provided for and live in bliss as a Master.

Angel EFT to open and balance the fifth dimensional Base Chakra

Visualise: The base of the spine where the base chakra is and see Archangel Gabriel place a ball of shimmering platinum energy into this chakra.

Take three deep breaths with hands by your sides or on the legs palms facing downwards if you are sitting.

HC: Archangel Gabriel please assist me now in opening and balancing my base chakra

TH: I easily command my needs from the benevolent and loving universe

TE: *No talking just breathe comfortable full breath as you feel the energy integrate*

EB: *Breathe comfortable full breaths*

SE: I am blissfully aware of my foundations and how loved I am on this planet

UE: *Breathe comfortable full breaths as you feel the energy integrate*

UN: *Breathe another comfortable full breath*

CH: I always have nourishment available to me, thank you

CB: I always have shelter available to me, thank you

Th: I always have money readily available, thank you

If: Thank you Archangel Gabriel for allowing me to know any new learning from my base chakra today

Mf: *Breathe comfortable full breaths as you feel the energy integrate*

Rf: *Breathe a comfortable full breath*

Bf: I am deeply loved and supported as a master

KC: Thank you Archangel Gabriel for my activated fifth dimensional base chakra

HC: I choose to live in bliss

Pause to allow the new energy to settle

Sacral (sexual) chakra

The sacral chakra at the fifth dimension is a point on the lower abdomen about 3-4 inches below the navel and is iridescent pink and is also overseen by Archangel Gabriel. The focus is sensuality and sociability.

Angel EFT to open and balance the fifth dimensional Sacral Chakra

Visualise: Archangel Gabriel placing a ball of lustrous pink light into your Sacral Chakra, about 3-4 inches below the navel, flooding it with divine love and tranquillity.

Take three deep breaths with hands placed on lower abdomen underneath the belly button palms facing in towards the body

HC: Archangel Gabriel please assist me now in activating and integrating my sacral chakra

TH: I allow all limiting cords keeping me tethered to others to dissolve now

TE: *Just breathe comfortable full breaths as you feel the energy integrate*

EB: *Breathe comfortable full breaths*

SE: I am open to giving and receiving love with tenderness in my life

UE: *Breathe a comfortable full breath as you feel the energy integrate*

UN: *Breathe comfortable full breaths*

CH: Love with tenderness

CB: Softness in my being

Th: I invite the flow of higher love

If: Thank you Archangel Gabriel for allowing me to know any new learning from my sacral chakra today

Mf: *No talking just breathe comfortable full breath as you feel the energy integrate*

Rf: *Breathe another comfortable full breath*

Bf: Love and transcendent sexuality

KC: Thank you Archangel Gabriel for my activated sacral chakra

HC: I allow the flow of higher love

Pause to allow the new energy to settle

<u>Navel chakra</u>

The navel chakra is a point just below the navel and is orange and is also overseen by Archangel Gabriel, and which helps us remove the blocks and boundaries to accepting others and living in oneness consciousness.

Angel EFT to open and balance the Navel Chakra

Visualise: See Archangel Gabriel placing a radiant ball of orange energy into your sacral chakra, just below the navel.

Take three deep breaths with hands placed on lower abdomen over the belly button palms facing in towards the body

HC: Archangel Gabriel please assist me now in activating and integrating my navel chakra
TH: Allowing judgements and limitations to dissolve as I open up to oneness
TE: *Breathe comfortable full breaths as you feel the energy integrate*
EB: *Breathe comfortable full breaths*
SE: I allow my sociability
UE: *Breathe comfortable full breath as you feel the energy integrate*
UN: *No talking just breathe comfortable full breaths*
CH: I bring forward sensuality
CB: Balanced in my being
Th: Sociability and sensuality
If: Thank you Archangel Gabriel for allowing me to know any new learning from my navel chakra today
Mf: B*reathe comfortable full breaths as you feel the energy integrate*
Rf: *Breathe another comfortable full breath*
Bf: I radiate light and connectedness to others
KC: Thank you Archangel Gabriel for my activated navel chakra
HC: Oneness

Pause to allow the new energy to settle

Solar Plexus Chakra

The solar plexus chakra is at a point just under where the ribcage meets and is overseen by Archangel Uriel. The colour is gold with rainbow lights. The focus is on your inner wisdom and knowledge.

Angel EFT to open and balance the fifth dimensional Solar Plexus Chakra

Visualise: Archangel Uriel placing a ball of gold with rainbow lights in the solar plexus centre. See yourself integrating all the knowledge you have attained on your soul's journey. Allow yourself to tune into universal wisdom.

Take three deep breaths with palms facing in towards the solar plexus

HC: Archangel Uriel please assist me now in activating and integrating my solar plexus chakra

TH: I now integrate all of the knowledge my soul has collected

TE: B*reathe comfortable full breaths as you feel the energy integrate*

EB: *Breathe comfortable full breaths*

SE: I am open to universal wisdom

UE: *Breathe comfortable full breaths as you feel the energy integrate*

UN: *Breathe another comfortable full breath*

CH: I allow my inner knowledge to shine

CB: I have access to universal knowing

Th: Settled and contented in my power

If: Thank you Archangel Uriel for allowing me to know any new learning from my solar plexus chakra today

Mf: *Breathe comfortable full breaths as you feel the energy integrate*

Rf: *Breathe a comfortable full breath*

Bf: I am open to my inner knowledge and wisdom

KC: Thank you Archangel Uriel for my activated solar plexus chakra

HC: I allow the flow of knowledge

Pause to allow the new energy to settle

Heart chakra

Archangel Chamuel oversees the heart chakra and the focus is on unconditional love and compassion.

Angel EFT to activate and integrate the fifth dimensional Heart chakra

Visualise: A point in the very centre of the chest and see Archangel Chamuel placing a ball of pure white energy there now. Feel pure unconditional love expand and radiate out.

Take three deep breaths at heart centre

HC: Archangel Chamuel please assist me now in activating and integrating my heart chakra
TH: I Am compassion
TE: *No talking just breathe comfortable full breath as you feel the energy integrate*
EB: *Breathe a comfortable full breath*
SE: I Am love
UE: *Breathe comfortable full breaths as you feel the energy integrate*
UN: *Breathe another comfortable full breath*
CH: Unconditional love flows through me and radiates out from my being
CB: I connect to the oneness of universal love and healing
Th: Thank you for this love and compassion
If: Thank you Archangel Chamuel for allowing me to know any new learning from my heart chakra today
Mf: *Breathe comfortable full breaths as you feel the energy integrate*
Rf: *Breathe a comfortable full breath*
Bf: I anchor unconditional love and compassion in my being and in my energy
KC: Thank you Archangel Chamuel for my activated heart chakra
HC: I Am love and compassion

Pause to allow the new energy to settle

Throat chakra

Archangel Michael oversees the throat chakra, and at the fifth dimension it is royal blue. You are assisted to communicate with angels and Masters at this level.

Angel EFT to open and balance the fifth dimensional Throat chakra

Visualise: Archangel Michael placing a ball of royal blue into the point at the base of the neck in the centre. Allow this ball of energy to light up, filling the throat chakra and lighting it up.

Take three deep breaths with palms resting lightly over the throat centre

HC: Archangel Michael please assist me now in activating and integrating my throat chakra
TH: I communicate clearly with angels and Masters
TE: *No talking just breathe a comfortable full breath as you feel the energy integrate*
EB: *Breathe comfortable full breaths*
SE: It is easy for me to express myself
UE: *Breathe comfortable full breaths as you feel the energy integrate*
UN: *Breathe another comfortable full breath*
CH: I enjoy these blessings
CB: I communicate easily and with love
Th: My communications emanate with courage
If: Thank you Archangel Michael for allowing me to know any new learning from my throat chakra today
Mf: *Breathe comfortable full breaths as you feel the energy integrate*
Rf: *Breathe a comfortable full breath*
Bf: I speak words of truth and love
KC: Thank you Archangel Michael for my activated throat chakra
HC: Anchoring this light in my being now

Pause to allow the new energy to settle

Third Eye Chakra

Archangel Raphael works with the third eye chakra. At fifth dimension it is a sparkling crystal colour.

Angel EFT to open and balance the fifth dimensional Third Eye Chakra

Visualise: Archangel Raphael placing a ball of sparkling crystal energy into the centre of the forehead. Take three deep breaths with palms resting lightly on the forehead

HC: Archangel Raphael please assist me now in activating and integrating my third eye chakra
TH: I see through the veils and dimensions with love
TE: *Breathe comfortable full breath as you feel the energy integrate*
EB: *No talking just breathe comfortable full breaths*
SE: I co-create divine abundance
UE: *Breathe comfortable full breaths as you feel the energy integrate*
UN: *Breathe another comfortable full breath*
CH: I see the divine perfection in all things
CB: I focus my thoughts easily and with love
Th: I am a centre for Divine wisdom and intuition
If: Thank you Archangel Raphael for allowing me to know any new learning from my third eye chakra today
Mf: *Breathe comfortable full breaths as you feel the energy integrate*
Rf: *Breathe a comfortable full breath*
Bf: I anchor my intuition and divine wisdom
KC: Thank you Archangel Raphael for my activated throat chakra
HC: I co-create abundance

Pause to allow the new energy to settle

Crown Chakra

Archangel Jophiel works with the crown chakra. At fifth dimension it is a sparkling crystal colour.

Angel EFT to open and balance the fifth dimensional Crown Chakra

Visualise: Archangel Jophiel placing a ball of sparkling crystal energy into the crown. Take three deep breaths with palms resting lightly on the crown

HC: Archangel Jophiel please assist me now in activating and integrating my crown chakra
TH: I accept the golden white light of wisdom into my being
TE: *Breathe comfortable full breaths as you feel the energy integrate*
EB: *No talking just breathe comfortable full breaths*
SE: I accept light from my soul
UE: *Breathe a comfortable full breath as you feel the energy integrate*
UN: *Breathe another comfortable full breath*
CH: I open myself to higher light
CB: I bring this light into my being and into my life for the benefit of all
Th: I accept the wisdom of Source
If: Thank you Archangel Jophiel for allowing me to know any new learning from my crown chakra today
Mf: *Breathe comfortable full breaths as you feel the energy integrate*
Rf: *Breathe a comfortable full breath*
Bf: I anchor this light into my being
KC: Thank you Archangel Jophiel for my activated crown chakra
HC: I Am that I Am

Pause to allow the new energy to settle

Causal Chakra

Archangel Christiel works with the causal chakra. It is a pure brilliant white colour and is located above and slightly behind the crown chakra. This is where you connect with the spiritual world, and receive stellar transmissions.

Angel EFT to activate and integrate the Causal Chakra

Visualise: Archangel Christiel placing a ball of brilliant white energy into the causal chakra.

Take three deep breaths with palms cupped and resting lightly at the back of the crown

HC: Archangel Christiel please assist me now in activating and integrating my causal chakra
TH: I connect with my angels, Archangels and high frequency guides
TE: *Breathe comfortable full breaths as you feel the energy integrate*
EB: *No talking just breathe comfortable full breaths*
SE: I open my awareness to stellar transmissions
UE: *Breathe comfortable full breaths as you feel the energy integrate*
UN: *Breathe another comfortable full breath*
CH: Thank you angels for this connection
CB: Thank you Archangels for this connection
Th: Thank you Ascended Masters for this connection
If: Thank you Archangel Christiel for allowing me to know any new learning from my causal chakra today
Mf: *Breathe comfortable full breaths as you feel the energy integrate*
Rf: *Breathe a comfortable full breath*
Bf: I anchor this higher connection into my being
KC: Thank you Archangel Christiel for my activated causal chakra
HC: I am always connected

Pause to allow the new energy to settle

Soul Star Chakra

Archangel Mariel works with the soul star chakra, which is a radiant magenta pink colour and is located six inches above the top of your head.

Angel EFT to activate and integrate the Soul Star Chakra

Visualise: Archangel Mariel placing a ball of radiant magenta pink energy into the soul star chakra. Feel your spiritual essence.

Take three deep breaths with palms facing one another about six inches apart and six inches above the crown

HC: Archangel Mariel please assist me now in activating and integrating my soul star chakra
TH: I embrace the essence of my spirit
TE: *No talking just breathe comfortable full breaths as you feel the energy integrate*
EB: *Breathe comfortable full breaths*
SE: I open my awareness to my soul's incredible wisdom
UE: *Breathe a comfortable full breath as you feel the energy integrate*
UN: *Breathe comfortable full breaths*
CH: I use this wisdom to allow my full potential
CB: My skills and talents to come forward
Th: The amazing abilities I have had in all of my lifetimes
If: Thank you Archangel Mariel for allowing me to know any new learning from my soul star chakra today
Mf: *Breathe comfortable full breaths as you feel the energy integrate*
Rf: *Breathe another comfortable full breath*
Bf: My higher self glows with light
KC: Thank you Archangel Mariel for my activated soul star chakra
HC: I give thanks for my spirit

Pause to allow the new energy to settle

Stellar Gateway Chakra

Archangel Seraphina and Metatron works with the stellar gateway chakra, which is golden orange and is located fifteen inches above the top of your head. This chakra connects us to the wisdom of the Monad, which is your soul family of which you are said to be of twelve, of which there are twelve groups making 144 from the original Monad. Almost like the higher self of the higher self.

Angel EFT to activate and integrate the Stellar Gateway Chakra

Visualise: Archangels Seraphina and Metatron placing a ball of golden orange energy into the stellar gateway chakra. Feel the oneness of all things and your connection with Source.

Take three deep breaths with palms facing one another about six inches apart and fifteen inches above the crown

HC: Archangels Seraphina and Metatron please assist me now in activating and integrating my stellar gateway chakra
TH: I embrace the oneness of all things
TE: *No talking just breathe comfortable full breaths as you feel the energy integrate*
EB: *Breathe a comfortable full breath*
SE: I feel my boundless connection to Source
UE: *Breathe comfortable full breaths as you feel the energy integrate*
UN: *Breathe another comfortable full breath*
CH: I see the bridge of light of my Antakarana linking me to Source
CB: I feel the bridge energising and glowing now
Th: Feeling so supported in this connection
If: Thank you Archangels Seraphina and Metatron for allowing me to know any new learning from my stellar gateway chakra today
Mf: *Breathe comfortable full breaths as you feel the energy integrate*
Rf: *Breathe another comfortable full breath*
Bf: I accept this golden orange light as my own personal sun shining above me
KC: Thank you Archangels Seraphina and Metatron for my activated stellar gateway chakra
HC: I Am Light

Pause to allow the new energy to settle

Tune in and make a note of anything you want to remember. Ground your energy and ask your angel to pull your aura and your chakras in close to the body to a level that is comfortable and appropriate for you.

Chapter Summary:

● Ascension work is about raising our vibration to the point of light and involves purifying and clearing our emotions and thoughts, so that our actions come from love, for the highest good. We radiate at a higher level which is joyous and free.

● Activating and integrating the 12 fifth dimensional chakras helps us on our ascension journey and connects us to our divine wisdom and mastery.

Bibliography & Further Reading

Bach, R (1970, 1994). Johnathon Livingston Seagull: A Story. Harper Thorsons.

Brennan, B (1987) Hands of Light; a guide to healing through the human energy field. Batam Books. New York.

Cooper, D & Whild, T (2015). The Archangel Guide to Ascension, 55 Steps to the Light. Hayhouse. London.

Cooper, D & Crosswell, C (2009). Ascension Through Orbs. Findhorn Press. Scotland.

Emoto, Masaru (2001). The Hidden Messages in Water. Beyond Words Publishing Inc. Hillsboro, Oregon.

Fléche, C (2001) The Biogenealogy Sourcebook, healing the body by resolving traumas of the past. Healing Arts Press. Rochester, Vermont.

Hartmann, S (2012). Energy EFT. Dragonrising. UK.

Hellinger & Hövel (1999). Acknowledging What Is; conversations with Bert Hellinger. Zeig Tucker & Theisen Inc. Phoenix.

Ortner, N The Huffington Post http://www.huffingtonpost.com/nick-ortner/emotional-freedom-technique_b_1349223.html

Sai Maa Lakshmi Devi (2005). Petals of Grace, Essential Teachings for Self Mastery. Humanity in Unity Press, Boulder, Colorado.

Virtue D (2004). Archangels & Ascended Masters, A guide to working and healing with divinities and deities. Hayhouse Inc. Carlsbad, California.

Weiss, B (1988). Many Lives, Many Masters: The True Story of a Prominent Psychiatrist, His Young Patient, and the Past-Life Therapy That Changed Both Their Lives. Fireside.

About the Author

Susan Browne is a Guild of Energists certified Energy EFT Trainer and Master Practitioner and has trained with the Diana Cooper Foundation in Angels, Ascension and Lemurian Planetary Healing. Her background is that of a Usui Reiki Master, qualified Nurse in Mental Health and an Accredited Counsellor. Originally from Warwickshire, England Susan has lived and worked in Ireland since 2000.

Susan has always been interested in healing and energy work, and has a love of meditation and crystals since childhood. She discovered in her counselling practise that Energy EFT and working with the angels served to speed up recovery and healing from problems, and move people fluidly towards their goals.

Susan has a YouTube channel where she demonstrates Energy EFT and Angel EFT, and you can follow her work at Light Life Learning on Facebook and Twitter.

www.angeleft.com

Light Life Learning

About The Guild of Energists - GoE

The Guild of Energists is the only organisation in the world that deals with reasonable, rational, provable modern energism.

We have personal membership for individuals who love energy for self help and personal advancement; there is professional membership for modern energists who work as coaches, counsellors, therapists and healers; and there is the trainer's membership for those who teach and train others in modern energy work.

Our members come from all walks of life, we are all real people together on an amazing journey of personal discovery and empowerment. We share insights and experiences through our online forums, newsletters, our print magazine, The Energist, and our conferences.

We welcome dynamic, clear thinking, success orientated people to come and join us and help us make the world a happier place. Then the world can't but help become a better place as well!

Further Information

- History of the GoE: GoE.ac/hog
- Join the GoE: GoE.ac/join
- GoE Courses: GoE.ac/courses
- Find a GoE Practitioner: GoE.ac/map